MW01385335

Ballots, Bloomers
&
Marmalade

The Life of Elizabeth Smith Miller

Vote!

By Norman K. Dann

Norman K Dann

Log Cabin Books   Hamilton, NY
2016

LOG CABIN BOOKS

HAMILTON, NY 13346

WWW.LOGCABINBOOKS.COM

COPYRIGHT © 2016 BY NORMAN K. DANN

All rights reserved. No part of this book may be reproduced, distributed,
or transmitted in any form or by any means, or stored
in a database of retrieval system without the
prior written permission of the publisher.

First Paperback Edition: February 2016

10 9 8 7 6 5 4 3 2 1

ISBN: 9780997325102

Book and Cover Design by Christine Munn

The publisher will donate a portion of the profits from sales of this book
to the National Abolition Hall of Fame & Museum in Peterboro, NY.
and to the National Women's Hall of Fame in Seneca Falls, NY.

To Dorothy Willsey-Dann

As my life-partner, Dorothy has been the spark of inspiration that ignited my research efforts, and more importantly, my desire to challenge my intellectual capabilities and to become a family-oriented person.

CONTENTS

PREFACE ——————— VI

CHAPTERS & PAGES

I. ——————— 7
BIRTH AND CHILDHOOD

II. ——————— 17
EDUCATION

III. ——————— 25
HEALTH ISSUES

IV. ——————— 27
MARRIAGE AND INCOME

V. ——————— 39
EARLY RESIDENCES

VI. ——————— 45
CHILDREN

VII. ——————— 59
RELIGION

VIII. ——————— 65
PERSONAL INTERESTS

IX. ——————————— 87
TRAVEL

X. ——————————— 93
LOCHLAND

XI. ——————————— 101
FOSSENVUE

XII. ——————————— 113
PHILANTHROPY

XIII. ——————————— 123
DRESS REFORM

XIV. ——————————— 151
POLITICAL INTERESTS

XV. ——————————— 177
FINAL DAYS

EPILOGUE ——————————— 181

ACKNOWLEDGMENTS —— 187

NOTES ——————————— 189

BIBLIOGRAPHY —————— 204

INDEX ——————————— 210

ABOUT THE AUTHOR —— 215

PREFACE

Since her death in 1911, very little has been written about the life of Elizabeth Smith Miller. As the daughter of a socially prominent and aristocratic family, she had ample opportunity to seek power and influence within the reformist circles in the nineteenth century, yet she chose to remain on the periphery of most reform issues. She preferred to study and teach on issues of domestic style and order, and leave the political skirmishes to others. She did work in the women's rights movement obliquely through her interest in dress reform, and in conjunction with the efforts of her daughter Anne Fitzhugh Miller regarding suffrage. Her elegant home in Geneva, New York was a gathering place for some of the front-line participants in the long battle for woman suffrage.

Whereas this book follows Elizabeth's life chronologically, some issues covered will overlap various time periods. I have used original quotations of Elizabeth and others who were part of her life in order to convey as accurately as possible the <u>feelings</u> as well as the ideas of those involved. Most of the sources used are original and previously unpublished.

ELIZABETH SMITH MILLER
1822-1911

I

Birth and Childhood

Life was enjoyable for 17-year-old Gerrit Smith at the "College on the Hill" in Clinton, New York in 1814.

Hamilton College was chartered in 1812, having been founded 19 years earlier as an academy for boys. It took four hours to make the 20-mile trip to Clinton from Gerrit's home in Peterboro, and he had mixed emotions about being away from his family. He loved and missed his mother, Ann, and wrote letters to her often, but he did not miss his arrogant and avaricious father, Peter. Gerrit was, however, dependent upon Peter to pay his expenses from the profits of his very lucrative land sales business.

Before graduating from Hamilton College in 1818, Gerrit had become engaged to the daughter of Azel Backus , the first president of the college. Wealtha Backus and Gerrit were married in January of 1819 and loved one another dearly. Tragically, Wealtha would die of encephalitis seven months later. Gerrit's grief for his "lovely star" lasted through many months of depression.

A bright spot in this tragic scenario was offered by a young woman Gerrit had met through Wealtha's family. Ann Carroll Fitzhugh was, in 1818 when he first knew her, the 13-year-old sister of Wealtha's brother Frederick's wife Rebecca Fitzhugh Backus. The Fitzhughs were a former slave-holding family from western Maryland who had opted out of slave owning and moved to central New York State where they became influential in the founding of the city of Rochester.

Three years after Wealtha's death, Gerrit and Ann married on January 3, 1822, just eight days before her 17th birthday. Ann became a quiet, faithful, and supportive wife—a valued partner for an aristocratic male in the nineteenth century. She encouraged and assisted Gerrit's active and radical social reform activity in movements for the abolition of slavery, women's rights, temperance, and several other causes by providing a graceful and hospitable environment for hundreds of visitors during their long marriage.

Their love bore fruit with the birth of Elizabeth Smith on September 20, 1822 at the home of Ann's maternal grandfather, Col. William Fitzhugh, at Hampton in Livingston County, New York. William had arrived in that area in 1800 with Col. Nathaniel Rochester and Major Charles Carroll. They purchased a one-hundred-acre tract of land at Geneva Falls, which eventually became the City of Rochester. Shortly after Elizabeth's birth, Gerrit, Ann and the baby moved back to the Smith family mansion in Peterboro. Peter Smith had retired in 1819 after his wife's death, and he sold the land sales business and the mansion to Gerrit. Peter moved to Schenectady for the remainder of his life. He died there in 1837.[1]

Small children faced a precarious set of health risks in the early 1800s. What we now see as routine childhood diseases were often killers. Vaccines were rare, antibiotics did not exist, and infectious drinking water was a common problem. The cause of cholera was not discovered until 1854. Ann and Gerrit had a total of seven children, only two of whom lived to adulthood.

At the age of two, Elizabeth was "an engaging little creature" who Ann thought resembled her grandfather Peter. When baby Elizabeth did become ill, Ann often took her to Rochester to be under the care of her Fitzhugh family. As Elizabeth recovered from "some illness" in July 1823 at the age of only nine months, Ann wrote to Gerrit saying, "All I can say of our dear baby would only make you more impatient to see her." Gerrit developed warm, loving relationships with his female children, but would have cold and antagonistic relationships with his sons as he tried to dominate and control them.

What worried Gerrit and Ann the most was an epidemic of smallpox prevalent in central New York in the early 1820s. When Ann was visiting Hampton again in late 1824, she had both Elizabeth and her new baby brother Fitzhugh, who was born on October 18, 1824, vaccinated against smallpox. The process of vaccination was new—introduced through the scientific work of Edward Jenner in 1798—and did not offer certainty of protection. She had told Gerrit,

> "there are a great many cases of smallpox [near Hampton].... I have had our dear babies vaccinated, but I cannot tell as yet whether it has taken or not."

By one month later at the end of December, she reported that "the dear children are very well and I think will entirely escape the smallpox."[2]

Ann also wrote that Fitzhugh "has grown much and begins to laugh and crow quite sweetly." Sadly, Fitzhugh would die of dysentery at the age of 12. Regarding Elizabeth, she wrote,

> "As for your little Perfection - she is the admiration of the whole country. We found it quite a difficult task to manage her, after being so spoiled by her father. However, Bet has partly promised to take her under her control, so I suppose, by the time you see her, she will be a reformed character."

Gerrit wrote back, "Tell Lib that I hope she will soon have the opportunity 'to sleep long wi[th] Papa.'"

By age three, Elizabeth had acquired the nickname of "Libby" and was exhibiting what her parents viewed as troublesome "manners." Ann worried that if Gerrit were to have sole charge of her, "you would have your hands full." As a housekeeper at the Smith estate, Betsey Kelty knew the family well, and had agreed to mentor young Libby. "I hope," said Ann, "that miss Lib's manners will be much improved under Betty Kelty's good management."[3]

Both parents loved being with their children. Ann was a religious, church-going person who worried that Gerrit was not. She hoped that he would become so: "For the sake of our children I think it best that we should go together."

Gerrit was away from home often on business and speaking engagements. At such times, he longed for his family. "[I am] lonely and homesick," he wrote from Albany. "I wish you were by my side. I am a poor Critter out of the circle of my wife and children." A week later he wrote,

"Oh how much I wish to see you all. That capering Nan (their third child) is sporting before the eye of my imagination – and how do my dear Fitzhugh and Elizabeth do? I hope they have rec[eived] my letters to them."

"[I miss] dear... Nan's laugh and Libby's round + earnest eyes + Pit's (Fitzhugh's) witchery."

On one occasion when Libby was two and Gerrit had just returned home,

"I had scarcely got into the house before Lib began to exclaim- 'what have you brought me Pa? Is your trunk locked?' + many similar questions. I soon made such a display of toys to her as made her dance for joy. Among them is a string of white... beads, which she wears constantly."[4]

Long rides to visit extended family members or for medical treatment were common in spite of slow and poor travel conditions. They visited a doctor in Richfield Springs for treatment of "sores" on the children. He treated them, Libby included, with a "powder of calomel every morning"—a compound of mercury and chlorine used as a fungicide. There were frequent and sometimes long visits to the Fitzhughs in Hampton, with Libby perhaps staying there alone. After a long visit at age six, Ann remarked on her arrival there, "I found Libby well and delighted to see me. She has grown tall and slim and I think her somewhat improved in manners." On the ride home, "Libby bore the ride extremely well, every now and then favoring us (unasked) with a few verses of 'Tis believed that this harp.' She was delighted to get home, but I have reason to regret that I did not leave her with you for the noise of so many children seems to bring on somewhat of her old irritability." At that time in the mid-1820s, Gerrit and Ann were caring temporarily in their home for some children of relatives.[5]

During the period between 1831 and 1835 (Elizabeth being eight to twelve years old), home life for the five-member Smith family was relatively happy. Elizabeth, Fitzhugh and Nanny played together as they grew up. Ann told Gerrit of their activities: They "are busily engaged in building their mill by the plum tree under our room window." Libby and her older visiting cousin Elizabeth Cady (later to marry Henry B. Stanton) in one of their pranks "filled huge syringes with milk and bombarded two sleeping relatives." They also used "liquid blacking... for ammunition, to the great detriment of some of the... furniture." Libby told her father that she and her "little girl" friends "are to hold an Abolition meeting" upstairs. She liked dolls also, and provided materials to "Mrs. Harvey" for making "a Doll bonnet."[6]

The children seem to have gotten along with one another well—perhaps following the example of their parents. Letters and poems express a great deal of respect among family members, and often refer to their "happy" times. Gerrit referred to Fitzhugh and Libby as being "by my side [with] Fitzhugh telling Libby about Nanny. Among the things he says, 'she is a little witch... and makes people do whatever she wants done.'" Perhaps there was a little sibling rivalry there.[7]

There were also difficult times. The children did get the usual childhood afflictions such as colds, and "ear eruption," and measles. And Libby was concerned about her parents' evaluation of her "bad manners." Ann encouraged her to "strive to overcome some fault each day that you live." Libby did aspire "to be a better girl than I have been."[8]

But as well as the good times, the tragedies to strike the Smith family in the mid-1830s were enormous. As mentioned earlier, Fitzhugh died on July 10, 1836 of dysentery. That was the second severe blow that Ann, Gerrit, and Libby had faced. By late 1833, Nanny was experiencing seizures. Ann told her husband in a letter from Rochester, "I have described her fits to Doctor Backus, and he thinks that she must have some disease of the brain, and that she should be under the care of some eminent physician." Just six months later she wrote, "I am greatly grieved to hear that our dear Ann (Nanny) has had another fit. I did not expect it so soon."

These events were causing Ann to experience dissonance about her faith in a benevolent God, and she tried to resolve it by understanding the family situation to be "God's will." Nanny died suddenly on April 21, 1835 due to complications from seizures. Ann and Gerrit must have wondered if Libby would be spared to live to adulthood. Ann's letter to Gerrit of September 5, 1835 ended with, "Kiss dear Lib for me." She was their only child now.[9]

Perhaps as an escape from the depressive grief of the Smith's Peterboro home, Libby and Ann spent May through September of 1836 with Libby's grandparents at Hampton near Rochester. Libby studied music there—probably piano lessons—and appears to have enjoyed it and done well. Ann reported that, "Dear Libby... gets on very nicely with her music. I only fear that her soul may suffer harm from the almost unbounded praise bestowed upon her."[10]

After a brief stay in Peterboro in the fall, their "escape" continued through the winter in Philadelphia. Libby had become sick with a cold in Peterboro in November, and enjoyed their trip to "the South." Ann indicated that "Libby is delighted with her new home.... She is very cheerful and I think on the whole better...." "Dear Lib feels perfectly at home, and her health... is improving fast. She... complains very little of her throat, and I think she grows fat." They rented a piano for Libby to use, and the building owner (Mrs. Shipley) would not allow them to place it in the parlor, so they "consented" to put it in their room, "thinking it right to deny ourselves to save the feelings of others." Always concerned about her expenditure of money, she told Gerrit, "Lib takes her first music lesson tomorrow from Mr. Stanbridge at $24 a quarter. Our cash grows low. I hope a new supply will come soon." Gerrit sent her $50.00. The puzzling point is why she did not have her own checkbook during travels. The probable answer is that it was not appropriate for a woman to be financially independent at that time—and Gerrit preferred to use the money he earned to benefit people less well-off than his family.[11]

They enjoyed the winter there while Gerrit spent the winter in Peterboro working at his land business. Ann and Libby found it odd that he could be happy there alone, but he always did prefer "the press of my business" to traveling away from his beloved Peterboro.

In Philadelphia, they enjoyed shopping, going to entertainment events, and visiting friends. The James Forten family in that city had become friends with the Smiths through their common interest in the abolition of slavery. James was a free African-American who had become a successful sail maker, and vice president of the American Anti-Slavery Association. He knew Gerrit, and was in agreement with him that the education of black people was an important step on their path to freedom and equality. Gerrit had inaugurated one of the first formal schools for blacks in Peterboro in 1834. James' wife Charlotte and Ann became friends also.

Their visit to the Forten home included a meal of antislavery products. A popular tactic of the antislavery movement in the 1830s was to boycott products made with slave labor. The Smiths were ardent supporters of this movement. On this day, they had some candy made with "free sugar" and wrapped with paper containing antislavery sayings such as, "Roast your slave coffee as you will; It smells and tastes of slavery still."

Following their visit, which other acquaintances had noticed, Ann was asked, "What *other* niggers were there?" She told Gerrit she was "greatly agitated" by this comment, and admitted to him that she still had difficulty suppressing her own racist feelings.[12]

Ann and Libby also visited Lucretia Mott in Philadelphia. "She is a very interesting woman," said Ann. "I am so sorry she is a Unitarian." Ann did have her biases. Just four years later in 1840, Lucretia Mott and the newly married Elizabeth Cady Stanton would meet at the World Anti-Slavery Conference in London and make plans to organize the first women's rights convention in the United States, in Seneca Falls, NY in 1848.[13]

On a personal note, Ann and Libby also enjoyed shopping in Philadelphia. It was winter there, and Ann told her husband that she needed more money for Libby's "new boots. Shoes do not keep her feet sufficiently warm. I keep thick woolen stockings on her feet with the insides sprinkled with red pepper." Foot warmers! Libby also needed "a muff and a new cloak," and they both needed some dentistry work. Gerrit obliged by sending money, but he always seemed reluctant to do so.

Regarding Libby's cold feet, Ann was creative. She bathed Libby's "feet in warm salt water every morning," and rubbed her back with "opodeldoc (a mixture of alcohol, soap, and camphor used as a liniment) or some other warming thing. I have a burgundy plaster just below the back of her neck. All of this must be done to bring about a better circulation to keep her feet warm."

Libby was not pleased with these processes but went along with it anyway, perhaps in respect for her mother. Libby wrote, "I enjoy myself very much indeed, and who could help it, situated as I am?" She liked being out of Peterboro for the winter, especially in a big city.[14]

Her interest in city life may seem puzzling, especially so because she grew up in rural, isolated Peterboro. But perhaps some of the powerful influences on her there helped to develop in her a tendency toward urbane sophistication.

From the moment of her birth she was exposed daily to liberal, educated people involved in radical thought and action. But they were at just one end of the social spectrum. Libby met at her home nearly every variety of person extant. She listened to and conversed with the matriarchal Native American Oneidas, political leaders and statesmen, temperance advocates, runaway slaves, poor people begging for help, inventors seeking financial support, vagrants looking for work, preachers, and Harriet Tubman! The parade of visitors to her house never ended. During 1841-1842, Libby recorded an average of 33 visitors per month, all of whom were cordially received.[15]

The list of abolitionists she met in Peterboro is long, and includes all of the important leaders. Gerrit Smith was, because of his liberal ideas, his money, and his philanthropy, the most powerful abolitionist in the country. He therefore attracted others such as William Lloyd Garrison, publisher of The Liberator in Boston, Frederick Douglass, publisher of The North Star in Rochester, and activists John Brown, Theodore Weld, William Goodell, James G. Birney, Beriah Green, and many more, including Henry B. Stanton. Their effect on Libby was as that of a prep school for human rights activism that primed her for the future women's rights movement.

One frequent visitor to the Smith home in this same period was a banker from the nearby village of Cazenovia named Charles Dudley Miller— Libby's future husband. We will learn much more about him later.

Certainly the atmosphere in which Libby was reared was one of open-minded acceptance and generosity. As one journalist put it, "an atmosphere... enlivened by endless and most animated arguments on the burning issues of the day."[16]

Both parents had an influence on Elizabeth that was positive, deep, and enduring. Gerrit was humble in spite of his potential for aristocracy. He actually treated every person as equal, and was able to either shed or manage social biases. He expressed his humbleness by claiming that a picture of him illustrated his best side—the outside. One visitor noted glowingly, "I am enjoying his hospitability, his attractive conversation, his benevolent manners, his generous spirit, and surely it must be a miserably stupid being who could see all this without having the better emotions, the better and holier aspirations of his soul awakened, quickened, and strengthened into higher intensity for a like spirit, a similar character."

After Gerrit's death, one who had followed his writings but met him only twice commented,

> "I feel under great obligation to him for his teachings and example. I believe they have had a beneficial influence upon my own life, and that of my family. I never loved another with whom I was so slightly acquainted as I loved him. He has been my... ideal of a great and good man for the past thirty-five years.... I feel that I have suffered a personal loss—and it seems to me strange."[17]

Ann also had a profound influence on Libby. Her letters reveal a sincere concern for Libby's social and moral development—maybe to the point of overdoing it—yet Libby was always tolerant. Acquaintances remembered Ann as a special person.

> "She was remarkable for intelligence, hospitality, and benevolence, and her conversational powers were of a high order. Her presence gave added dignity and grace... to a home which will be remembered with delight by whoever entered it, and especially by the poor, the homeless, and the fugitive."[18]

When Ann and Libby visited the Fortens in 1836, Sarah Forten wrote, "Mrs. S[mith] is one of the plainest women in her dress I ever saw. I learn that she devotes nearly <u>all</u> of her income to benevolent purposes. This is so praiseworthy that I could not forbear to mention it to you. She is also one of these lovely good-natured women who takes one's heart on the instant." With such high quality parental influence, it is not surprising that Elizabeth grew into a liberal-minded, benevolent person.[19]

Yet as well as learning concern for others, she also learned the enormous importance of a supportive family. They wrote thousands of touching letters to each other when apart, and hundreds of love-filled poems that they compiled into a "Verse Book." Gerrit said of them,

"These rhymes will be prized by our successors because they will reveal one of the ways in which the members of our family sought to interest + gratify each other, + thus one of the ways of enabling them to form opinions of the tastes, habits, + character of our family."

Gerrit quipped about his own share of this work,
    "I crawl on earth's surface + be in its dust
    Asham'd that my soul will not soar.
    I try to write Stanzas—but oh they are just
    Most wretched of rhymes—nothing more."[20]

Elizabeth referred to the mutual love within their family as "oceans of love," and when someone neglected to express it in letters, or touches, or poems, others reacted with curiosity. "Why does not Libby write?" asked Gerrit while on a trip away from home. He hoped she would write to himself and to her former home-based nurse Laura Bosworth. "The thought that, as she grows up, she will decline in her love for the precious woman to whom she owes so much, is very painful to me. I should as soon she would forget me as her faithful nurse."[21]

If her parents had a huge influence on Libby's development, so did another major force: her formal education.

II

Education

Obviously the "general education" of any person starts in the womb and continues until death. We have already noted many of the early stimulants on Elizabeth Smith's development. Her formal education through hired professional teachers began in the early part of 1831 at her home in Peterboro.

Gerrit and Ann hired Miss Bell Wickham to tutor eight-year-old Elizabeth and six-year-old Fitzhugh. Gerrit queried Ann from Albany in late March, "How is Miss Wickham? I feel a great obligation to her for her faithfulness to our dear children.... I do think that very few children, at the age of ours, are further advanced... in what may be regarded as the useful education of a child." And five days later,

> "Tell dear Libby and Pit that... I hope they are making rapid improvement under Bell's tuition." Gerrit expressed appreciation for Bell's "affectionate care," and was pleased with Libby's "late improvement."[1]

The young Elizabeth certainly internalized her father's life-long concern for the importance of education. In 1834 she observed his efforts at the establishment of a school in Peterboro for black males, telling her grandfather,

> "They have all been preparing things for the black school which is to be held in [Peterboro]."[2]

Elizabeth's second hired tutor was Caroline Freedom King. She tutored Libby sometime between 1832 and 1834. Born in Hamilton, NY on May 22, 1810, King pursued a long professional career in education. After her initial teaching experience in Peterboro, she worked as a "preceptress" (administrator) and teacher at schools in Lafayette (1836), Fayetteville (1840), and Cherry Valley (1843), all in New York. In 1845, Caroline moved to Troy and became a student for one year at Emma Willard's Troy Female Seminary. She accepted a teaching position there in 1846 that lasted until 1872, after which she taught for a brief time at Evans Academy in Peterboro. Libby liked Caroline King and stayed in touch with her regarding later academic endeavors. Caroline valued her Peterboro experience, writing to Gerrit from Lafayette in 1836,

"I think of my dear Peterboro friends very often... and feel the want of their society more now... than at any time since I left that dear village."[3]

In May of 1835, Elizabeth enrolled in the Rev. Dr. Hiram H. Kellogg's Young Ladies Domestic Seminary in Clinton, NY. He was a classmate of Gerrit Smith at Hamilton College and a graduate of both Hamilton College and Auburn Theological Seminary. He became an active abolitionist and opened his school in 1833 as a manual labor school in which students spent part of their time working for the institution. Libby reported, "I work in the dishes.... I washed the dishes this morning and most all of them this noon." While in attendance there for one year she roomed with a person she called "Miss Mygatt." They must have been compatible, for Libby registered no complaints. Miss Mygatt is also referred to as "Minny," and is connected to "cousin" Ellen Cochrane Walter, Gerrit's sister's daughter. Gerrit signed a letter to Libby and Minny as "Yr. aff. father + uncle."[4]

The curriculum at the seminary included "French, philosophy, and arithmetic." Ann wrote to her daughter often, almost always enclosing some form of moral counseling. She warned against idleness: "Life is too short to let an hour pass without improving our minds and hearts...." There were frequent reminders to "love Jesus," to "speak evil of no one," to "walk in the truth," to keep "the heart fixed on Christ," and the like. Libby took such moralizing well even though she was skeptical of her own religious faith.[5]

Ann also monitored Libby's attitude, and even her spelling.

"There are... two words spelled wrong—<u>comeing</u> and <u>wipeing</u>. You see the mistake... you will never spell them so again."

Clearly, Ann had difficulty letting go. And regarding attitude,
"We hope to find you improved much in head and heart.... But the heart is the main thing. Do see to it that [it] be filled more and more in the love of Jesus. This is true knowledge."[6]

When Ann and Gerrit traveled to Clinton to visit Libby, they also went on to Utica to see Fitzhugh who was attending school there.[7]

One issue that Libby dealt with while at Clinton was homesickness. In May of 1835 she was only 12 years old and had not been away from home and parents for an extended time before this. Her mother noted,
"I am sorry you have been so low spirited."

And the Smiths' housekeeper Betsey Kelty advised,
"I hope you have gotten over your homesickness. I think you had better indulge as little as possible in gloomy and low spiritual feelings—not that I would recommend to you to be giddy and trifling, but there is a way to be composed and cheerful by having the heart fixed on Christ."[8]

This appears to be superb advice to one who was having mental (head) battles over the dissonance between her weak religious faith and the moral advice of her parents. Emotional balance, advised Kelty, could be achieved by just loving people (heart).

Yet in spite of Libby's developing need for independence, Mom could not stop nagging.
"I hope you have mended your dress. Be particular my dear to keep everything about you in nice order, teeth especially.... Do take good care of your health; wear thick shoes and stockings to school."

And get over "those turns of trembling. They are somewhat of a nervous affection." Trust in the "Great Physician." Ann probably felt good that Libby had to attend "worship" each morning.[9]

As the year's schooling progressed, Libby felt better. "I am not home-sick," she announced. Her teachers had expressed pleasure with her "cheer-ful" attitude, and she looked forward to coming home for a visit. But Mom told her that she would be

> "home for so short a time that we shall want all your company to ourselves. So papa and I have concluded that you must not go out any to <u>little girl parties</u>...."

She even reassured her Mom that

> "I have attended to your directions for two nights... about cleaning my teeth."[10]

Just before her year at the seminary ended in May of 1836, Libby con-fided to her parents, "I thank you... for being so kind to me when I was so low spirited. I am glad that I remained [in school], and hope that I shall make rapid progress.... Je suis contente avec ma situation."[11]

She took her contentedness to Rochester for the summer of 1836 for a five-month visit with the Fitzhugh family. While there she relaxed, studied music, and asked her father to buy her a piano for her birthday. About a year later, Libby reported to her former governess Caroline King regarding her successful and busy life.

> "My studies, my work, my wardrobe, and many unanswered letters, all combined, cry aloud to me for the distribution of justice. Some are omitted, others delayed, and many hang as dead weights on my time."

During 1838, Libby spent most of her time in Peterboro. Her parents intended "to get a lady who could teach Lib music and French," but that probably did not happen. Her next serious attempt at academic work came in late 1839 in Philadelphia.[12]

By November 8, 1839, Ann and Libby were in Philadelphia for the purpose of Libby's attending school. They first sought admittance to "Miss Hawk's" school, but learned that Ann and Libby could not live together because Libby's residence at the school was required. She was accepted at Hannah Whitall's Quaker school. Opened in 1823, it operated until Han-nah married in 1845. The school term ran from November to April. Ann stayed with Libby until just before Christmas at which time she returned to Peterboro. They rented a place with "Miss Bullock" on North Eighth Street. Ann commented, "I pay Miss Bullock every Thursday morning."[13]

Back in Peterboro, Gerrit and "Aunt Betsey" Kelty missed Ann and Libby. Betsey even went to Libby's room to try to experience her presence—an indication of the significance of "family" ties in the Smith household.[14]

Just before Libby's classes started in the second week of November, Ann said that they were "fixed for the winter" in their apartment, but had one worrisome concern. Libby was experiencing chronic back pain.

> "I hope the dear child will be able to study. I very much fear that the pain between her shoulders comes from an affection of the spine. I find one spot of great tenderness just where the pain is."

The pain became intense enough for her to seek medical advice.

> "Lib is seeing [Dr.] Lingen about her back pain.... [He] recommends she lighten her academic load."

The source of the pain was not determined, and it was not mentioned again during her six-month stay in Philadelphia.[15]

Classes ran daily 9:00 AM to 2:00 PM. Libby's lessons included scripture (Bible study), chemistry, arithmetic, geometry, composition and grammar, history of England and France, and a two-hour guitar lesson every other day. She liked the music, and considered

> "her music lesson and practice as recreation, and makes rapid improvement."[16]

After three weeks of study, it was evident that Libby's workload was too great. She tried to balance the use of her time by setting aside one hour for walking each day. Also, with her mother's encouragement, she dropped the study of history. Gerrit wrote that he hoped "her head and heart are... cleansed of all notions about rides + parties... + that she is bent on being a woman of sense + spirituality." As he did with all his children, he could not help but impose his values onto her—perhaps in part because he was paying the bills. At one point, due to the "Panic of 1837"—a deep economic depression that continued into the early 1840s—he even advised them to

quit. "I shall find it difficult to keep you and Libby at Philadelphia—difficult even to get money enough to visit you. [So] simply to save the expense
[please return to Peterboro]."[17]

They did not.

After Ann left Philadelphia in late December, her letters contained
seemingly contradictory notions. While she poured forth emotions regarding how much she missed Elizabeth, she also loaded onto Libby responsibilities that were not related to her studies. The emotions:

"I do, indeed, desire to see you, my dear, more than I can express.
We were so long together in Phil. depending on each other for our
happiness so much, that now I am removed from you I feel quite lost."

And again,

"I cannot tell you my dear child how much I want to see you. I feel
as if I should enjoy your society if we live to be again united more than
ever before." And she chastised Libby for not writing letters often
enough. Perhaps Libby was busy at school![18]

Then, regarding responsibilities:

"Write straighter; you need improvement in the formation of your
capitals; do take good care of your health; I do pray... that you may be
preserved from the fascinations of this present world."

Ann also instructed Libby to go shopping for her and bring to Peterboro a few items on her next visit. The list included

"the finest linen thread, a pound of the best arrow root, a dozen
vanilla beans, a pound of knitting cotton, 10 yds. of blue cloth, 12 yds.
of calico, 9 yds. of India camlet, and 18 yds. of dark calico."

Ann closes her requests with, "Take courage. [All this work] will help
you to be a woman of business." One wonders if Libby needed to be both a
serious student and a woman of business simultaneously. And how was she
to lug all that stuff home? Ann signed her letter "Your attached mother."
That is a very revealing admission. Attachments today are perceived more
as anchors than aids.[19]

The winter/spring portion of Elizabeth's Philadelphia schooling was relatively uneventful. She did make a late February visit to Peterboro. Gerrit's business clerk in Peterboro, Caleb Calkins, was sent to Philadelphia to help Libby prepare for the train trip to Wampsville, NY. There was some concern about money, although Gerrit did continue to pay the bills, and Ann continued to "write a little (four page letters!) by way of relief" for not being with Libby. "Are you surprised," Ann asked, "at the frequency of my epistles?"[20]

Before she left for home, Libby and Minny spent some recreational time in Germantown—an independent borough six miles northwest of the center of Philadelphia founded in 1681 by Quaker families. It was absorbed into the city in 1854. Being concerned about Libby's studies, Ann quipped, "When the cat's away the mice will play. I dare say you did not feel much like study...." I wonder what they did there. Ann wanted to know "if you are able to pursue all the studies you had when I left you." In spite of Libby's assurances that she was doing well without Mom, Ann still wondered, "Have you time to darn your stockings?"[21]

Although Elizabeth's formal education stopped in 1840, she never abandoned the student mentality. In 1843, due to Gerrit's near economic insolvency, she worked as a clerk in the Peterboro Land Office and learned the land business trade. She worked for decades learning about cooking and other domestic issues, becoming a mentor to thousands who read her 1875 book In The Kitchen. In the early 1860s she took horse riding lessons, had "an excellent German teacher," and a "French teacher," and did some translating work between English and French. She also took lessons in drawing at "the Academy of Design" in New York City, and during the 1870s and 1880s learned techniques of effective political networking with the aid of her daughter.[22]

Near the end of her life, Libby consummated her life-long efforts for the education of women by helping to motivate Geneva businessman William Smith to found William Smith College, and by helping to fund some of its costs.

Before moving on to cover Elizabeth's marriage, income, and domestic issues, we'll take a quick look at some general health issues that were a part of her life.

III

Health Issues

The issues of health faced by Elizabeth Smith Miller during her long life seem amazingly minor compared to those faced by many people during the 1800s, even members of her own family. Her brother Greene suffered intense pain from what is recognized today as fibromyalgia, and died of tuberculosis at age thirty-eight. Brother Fitzhugh died at age 12 of dysentery; sister Ann at age five of seizures; and three other siblings—Henry, Katie, and an unnamed child—all died in infancy.

Perhaps the most frequent problem faced by all people in the 1800s was "disordered bowels." There are many letters in which Elizabeth is cited with that difficulty. "We intended to take the boat tonight for home," wrote Ann, "but yesterday afternoon and through the night dear Lissie has been quite unwell with looseness of the bowels attended with much pain" (1846). And, "I hope you are quite recovered from the dysentery" (1852). As early is 1833, Ann wrote, "I feel no little alarm about the cholera...." As treatment she used "mustard poultices" and "bands of old flannel... around the stomach." Such "cures" did not help, and the problem persisted until the cause was clearly understood in the 1860s.[1]

Libby also had her share of colds, with the most frequent written complaint being a sore throat. Other non-life threatening ailments she endured were measles and whooping cough, and probably others that were not recorded. One serious health battle she had occurred in 1844.[2]

In early October, Libby had a well-advanced case of mastitis in one breast. Mastitis is a staph infection of breast tissue that causes redness, swelling, and pain, and, if not properly treated, can form an abscess and hemorrhage. Although it usually occurs in lactating women, that is not a necessity. Libby described her symptoms as follows:

> "I am no worse than I was yesterday morning, + perhaps have not quite as much pain.... I felt drowsy this morning, probably owing to opium. The hemorrhage still continues, but, I think, does not increase."

She also experienced fever and periodic chills.

In the 1840s mastitis was called "ague in the breast," and there was no effective treatment. Today, antibiotics can quell the infection within one day, but Libby suffered with it until it had run its natural course, probably lasting for several months. Ann went to Libby's Cazenovia home to care for her in October, and during the winter Libby hired a full-time attendant— Mrs. Burwell. Their treatment involved consumption of liquids, and the application of ice to help control swelling.[3]

Libby did recover, and certainly had to have been of strong physical constitution to survive such a serious infection. Her mother summed it up by writing, "What a peck of troubles you have been in, my darling—an ague of the breast, and so many little things to try you." The "big things" in her life—marriage, houses, and children—were yet to come.[4]

IV

Marriage and Income

While Elizabeth was still living in the Peterboro mansion with her parents, she kept a lot of records of what happened with the family. There are lists of food items purchased and prices paid, hardware items for maintenance of the estate, sewing items for making clothes, and—most importantly—a list of numbers of visitors to the estate with some names recorded.

THE SMITH MANSION, WHERE ELIZABETH LIVED WITH HER PARENTS UNTIL HER MARRIAGE TO CHARLES MILLER IN 1843, THEN AGAIN FROM 1846 TO 1850. BUILT BY PETER SMITH IN 1804, THE MANSION BURNED IN 1936. *FROM THE AUTHOR'S COLLECTION*

In the year 1842 she noted 132 visitors. During that year, one name appeared more frequently than any other. Charles Dudley Miller was the cashier of the Madison County Bank in the village of Cazenovia—10 miles west of Peterboro—and he was courting Elizabeth.[1]

Charles was born in Utica, NY on December 3, 1818. He was the eighth child of Hon. Morris S. Miller, and his wife Maria Bleeker, an organizer of the Dutch Reformed Church in Utica, NY. A 1798 graduate of Union College, Morris Miller was the private secretary to Governor John Jay. He opened a law practice in Utica in 1806, was elected president of the Village of Utica in 1808, and became judge of the Court of Common Pleas of Oneida County in 1810, a position he held until his death in 1824. He was also elected as a Federalist to the 13th U.S. Congress in 1813. Obviously Charles came from a socially prominent family, and was viewed by the Smiths as an appropriate suitor for Elizabeth. Gerrit was certainly pleased with his business acumen, and Ann was impressed with "his sweet words (which are heartfelt) about my dear Lissie." In letters to Elizabeth, she would sign off with,

"Give a sweet kiss to dear Charles for me."[2]

CHARLES DUDLEY MILLER RIDING IN A CARRIAGE.
COURTESY OF HOBART & WILLIAM SMITH COLLEGES

Elizabeth and Charles planned a wedding for October 1843, and as the date approached, both Elizabeth and her father had some guidelines in mind. Libby informed Charles that he must not require her to do things that she did not wish to do—a precursor to her future interest in women's rights issues. And Gerrit, just two months before the October 18 wedding, informed her of his expectations for it. They were traveling from Albany to Peterboro after having been in New York City for treatment of Gerrit's eyes when he counseled her regarding a proper wedding. Having been reared to think for herself, Libby was surprised about her father's instructions. As Gerrit related the incident to Ann:

> "She expressed her surprise last evening to my opposition to a fashionable wedding. She will, however, on reflection, be convinced that it belongs to the class of things which God hates. It seems to me, that I could never drag my reluctant feet again to a fashionable wedding: and to have one in my own family would be to violate if not to make void, our long standing example of belief in simplicity.... Should our Elizabeth ever be married, my taste would be to have the ceremony take place in the presence of none but the family of her lover + her own family: and I would prefer the ceremony followed by a good breakfast to be partaken of by the two families.... I should, in a word, wish the wedding to be an event that would please God, however much it might disgust a fashion-bound world."

CHARLES DUDLEY MILLER AND ELIZABETH SMITH MILLER

MASSACHUSETTS HISTORICAL SOCIETY   AUTHOR'S COLLECTION

Libby expressed the flavor of her own independence by writing in this same letter,

> "His notions of a wedding do not agree with mine. What is the harm of having your relatives together at that time, more than at any other? As to Father's proposition, I don't fancy it, + am pretty sure Charlie's friends would not, but I shall not trouble myself about it."[3]

She was not going to risk her own balance by worrying about Gerrit's biased opinions.

The wedding took place at "The Grove"—a temporary home for the Smith family about a mile south of the hamlet of Peterboro that was being used while Gerrit tried to sell the Peterboro mansion to maintain solvency during the Panic of 1837. It was evening time when the Rev. Beriah Green, an abolitionist friend of the Smith family, performed the service. Present were just the immediate families of the bride and groom plus two friends of Charles.[4]

Betsey Kelty provided a description of the bride as looking

> "very sweet in her simple white muslin without 'gold or pearls' + nothing on her head save her black glossy hair [and] a little bunch of white [Christmas] rose + green geranium [leaves] stuck in her comb. As they stood up together they were... very lovely looking specimens of humanity. Then in about an hour... they had a supper in the little dining room where the water runs. All the supper was cold except the tea + coffee. Mr. Smith was quite sick with a cold... but was as cheerful as he could be + Mrs. Smith praised herself... for getting through the evening without crying...."

In his typical business-like style, Gerrit warned the newlyweds on their wedding day to stay out of debt because it produces so much unhappiness, then he offered her any furniture she wanted from the mansion.

For their honeymoon, "they left the next morn before daylight to take the cars (train) for Schenectady, Albany, N York, Boston, etc., and were gone three weeks + then returned looking very well...." No record exists of their honeymoon trip, which is probably as it should be. On their return, they stayed for one day with the Smiths at The Grove, then moved into their own home in Cazenovia. Ann was pleased with their relationship, but still had to dispense advice. "I am very happy to hear that you and dear Charlie are so happy in each other. God grant that this happiness may be a deepening stream.... Be <u>sure</u>, my dear children, that you are 'new creatures' in Christ Jesus." Such advice was politely ignored. Neither of them was inclined toward religion.[5]

To develop our knowledge of Charles a bit more, it is interesting to note that he was called "Colonel Miller" for most of his life. Shortly after their move to Cazenovia, he joined a company of militia of the National Guard, 129th regiment, and was commissioned as Colonel by Governor Seward.[6]

In April of 1846, Charles resigned as cashier of the Madison County Bank, and became director of that bank two months later. He worked intermittently as a clerk for Gerrit Smith in his Peterboro Land Office, and was variously listed in census data as a "retired banker," "retired farmer," or "gentleman." After marriage, he did not need to work at an occupation for pay because—as we shall see—the Miller family income was guaranteed through a relationship with Gerrit. During his various short periods of work for Gerrit, their relationship was tense. Charles would coldly inform Gerrit of business projects or debt collections in process, and sometimes receive Gerrit's criticism. In one exchange, Gerrit wrote, "You have replied to my charges very successfully. May we both get rid of our conceit."[7]

His lack of a steady job did allow Charles to be somewhat of a "utility infielder" and take on jobs as needed, but it also led to charges of him being lazy. Greene once said of him and Libby after they had moved to a new home in Geneva, "Sister looks tired. She works too hard; but the Prince Consort has not injured himself by labor as yet." Charles even said of himself, "I think too much, + act too little."[8]

His religious skepticism bothered the Smith family. Ann mused, "I know it requires no small degree of self-denial for Charlie to go [to church] and hear [a minister] every Sunday...." She felt that shared religion would help them develop a strong bond.

> "My children—my heart longs after you with tears, that Charlie may be 'born again' + that Lissie may come under a fresh baptism of the Holy Ghost—that you may be <u>inseparably</u> one."

Actually, they shared a <u>lack</u> of interest in religion, which might have created its own bond. Betsey Kelty wondered about Charles,

> "I am unable to decide for myself... whether he is a Christian or not. He is very amiable + affectionate... + I should hope he would yield very readily to the best influences...." Betsey and Ann knew, of course, what those "best influences" were, but Charles was not ready to "yield."[9]

In general terms, Charles was a peaceful and benevolent person who seemed to prefer his own company to that of most others. For example, six years after their 1869 move to Geneva, Elizabeth and her daughter Anne developed a camp on the shore of Seneca Lake called Fossenvue. Its intellectual endeavors, as we shall learn later, attracted many impressive visitors. Charles "could seldom be coaxed to honor the camp with his presence even for a day, preferring, as he did, the comforts of his own Lochland (home) to the discomforts of [Fossenvue]" which he called "fuss in view."[10]

Charles was recognized publically as being "kindly, sympathetic, [and] helpful to fellow men in distress. The deserving who were in need were never turned from his door empty-handed." "He was charitable. His ready assistance was always kindly given in personal service... to public efforts for charitable objects.... He was peaceful. No quarrel or litigation ensued even when his cherished projects and pleasures were invaded.... Having been trained as a banker, he was... just and exact, so occasions of contention were avoided."[11]

Charles wrote long and loving poems to family members on special days that are now collected in the Verse Book. Gerrit recognized in verse Charles' passion for horses in an 1848 Christmas poem:

> "There's Charlie, that lover of all that is <u>hoss</u>,
> Give him something to suit him, oh dear Santa Claus!
> Or, if you have nothing that's <u>hoss</u>-like for him,
> Have you not what is swamp-like, to suit his swamp whim?
> Give him something you must—the best that you can—
> For Charlie is a noble + true hearted man."

Charles was reputed to have kept a beautiful stable for his personally raised Russian thoroughbred horses.[12]

CHARLES WAS REPUTED
TO HAVE KEPT A BEAUTI-
FUL STABLE FOR HIS PER-
SONALLY RAISED RUSSIAN
THOROUGHBRED HORSES.
*COURTESY OF GENEVA
HISTORICAL SOCIETY*

Other recreational interests in Charles' life included fishing, playing
some type of music, and stage acting. Libby commented about "the Play.... I
went last night + enjoyed it greatly. Charlie acted admirably."[13]

The marriage relationship between Charles Dudley Miller and Elizabeth Smith Miller had some typical "ups and downs" during its 53 years.
During their courtship, Elizabeth wondered if she should even get married,
and discussed the issue with her friend Kate L. Howe at Peterboro in July of
1841. Kate offered some poetic advice:

> "Oh why should a woman ever love,
> Throwing her charm away
> Her little chance of happiness
> On a rainbow ray....
>
> May you remain the same,
> Unchanged, except in name."

Obviously Kate was not optimistic about marriage. Why, she asked, should a woman throw away her chance for a happy life on a dream? In the early 1840s, marriage for a woman meant the loss of independence and property as well as her own name. Elizabeth did show a gleam of independence by always maintaining "Smith" as a part of her name. One of the first women to protest the potential loss of independence and name was Lucy Stone when she married Henry Blackwell on May 1, 1855.[14]

Just after the wedding, Ann was optimistic about their relationship. She loved Charles, even to the point of suggesting that he had "taken the place in my heart which my dear departed son would have had." Although she missed having Libby at the Smith estate daily, she felt assured that they would be happy together. But all was not well with the newlyweds.[15]

Just three months after the wedding, Libby was depressed. The issue was Charles' dominance of her and the home. Her mother sympathized with Libby's "peculiar trials," for she also identified with them. "You have my sympathy especially, for I went through the same in the first years of my marriage—afraid to have things in the house as I wanted them—in short—afraid to be mistress in my own house...." Then she advised, "Now, my darling, is a glorious time for you to take the reins into your own hands.... Be gentle, firm,... composed, as if all around you were pleased with it.... Your precious husband will be pleased...." Well, at least she hoped so. Libby must have been having a difficult time, for her need for domestic order—as we shall see later—was very high. Ann recommended that "housekeeping will be a remedy for many of your difficulties. In the meantime keep your spirit quiet... and perform 'the dear tasks of life'... with joyfulness as far as possible." She did not see Charles as being at fault, and blamed their early marital difficulties on Libby. "Kiss dear Charlie for me. I thank and love him more and more for his gentleness and patience with your peculiarities. You will overcome, my darling, I am sure."[16]

But Elizabeth was not so sure. She was questioning the future of their relationship, and asked her husband, "I wish I could realize your love for me—did what I said of its dying away trouble you?" She accused him of just trying to please her instead of honoring and respecting her, and that such efforts "were for what you imagined me to be. Now you are beginning to

<u>know</u> me... and if my fears are well grounded, you must tell me...." She felt that her expressions of her own needs and independence were bothering Charles, and that he was becoming remote and withdrawn. "You must expect your 'Pussie' [to be] troublesome, but as you are to take her 'for better or worser' you must learn to bear all things."[17]

Evidently Charles did "bear all things" well, for their relationship survived. During the decades of the 1850s-1870s they managed issues well, although the relationship did become somewhat cold and distant. Instead of loving and affectionate salutations in letters, Libby signed off with just "Farewell, Lissie." Yet their four children seemed happy and were a source of parental pride. Charles wrote poetically on their anniversary in 1859:

> "Back sixteen years ago they say,
> Young you and I did wed each other,
> Four precious milestones mark the way
> One little girl, and three to brother.
> Say! Aren't we happier now, than then?"

Actually, he did not sound too sure about that happiness.[18]

Then, near the end of their marriage, Charles lamented what appears to be Elizabeth's dying love:

> "Dear Lizzie! As I learned and listened
> To your <u>call</u>, no foolish tear
> Of sudden impulse glistened,
> Nor sign of pain, or joy, or fear—
> It was so soft yet strong
> I could not bear to move
> When it was done, for love
> Had whispered through it all
> To <u>me</u> 'she sings farewell.'"

This is an immensely powerful verse. Charles starts off shocked: "Dear Lizzie!" He is staggered. Has he heard this right? Not wanting to be sure, he exclaims, "Dear Lizzie!" He had quietly "learned and listened" to her concerns about an evidently fruitless relationship. Her "call" to end it stunned him so that no "sudden impulse... of pain, or joy, or fear" made any sense to him. She was "so soft yet strong" that he was paralyzed and could not "move when it was done." Elizabeth's "love... Had whispered... farewell."[19]

This verse was written in late 1884, and they did not part for the remaining 11 years of their relationship, but it must have been stagnant. Had divorce been as legitimate in the popular mind as it is now, I believe they would have done it—especially given Libby's lifelong orientation toward female independence and power. But that is just speculation, and the fact is that they stayed together "until death did them part."

Charles died "suddenly and unexpectedly" on February 2, 1896 at Lochland, probably of a heart attack. Ten years later, Elizabeth donated a portrait of him as a young man to Harvard College.[20]

An interesting feature of their long relationship involves their income. Neither of them was in tune with tenets of frugality, so they spent money lavishly on both themselves and others. When Gerrit remarked that they were too extravagant during one of their trips, Charles replied that they would "not be harmed by being a little more careful...." Why was Gerrit concerned? A look at the source of their income will answer that question.[21]

For most of their adult lives, neither Charles nor Elizabeth had a regular paying occupation. The reason for that is clear: Gerrit supplied them with an annual income of $8,000. We should note that an average annual income for one person during the 1840s was approximately $500. Gerrit's annual income from rental property and land sales was usually in the hundreds of thousands of dollars, and he was proud that "one of the greatest joys of my life has been to supply my wife + children with the means for making things... comfortable."

And that he did. The Millers' "annual allowance" was received quarterly, and in cases where extra money was needed, Gerrit sent smaller amounts as well. In her "Common Place Book," Elizabeth recorded many such amounts "received from Father." And when Libby or Charles or Ann traveled, Gerrit would pay those expenses, also. At one point, Gerrit had over 2,000 open land sales accounts, and collected annual rental fees of $40,000 to $60,000 from property on the Oswego waterfront alone. Payments received by the Millers sometimes exceeded $8,000 per year. In late

1870, Libby asked Gerrit, "how much [have I] received from you beyond the promised $8,000?" Their income "year" ran from July 1 through June 30, and if Gerrit was delinquent in meeting his payments to them, they wrote to ask for it. On an east coast trip between Boston and Nova Scotia in August of 1871, Libby wrote to Gerrit, "keep writing + give us plenty of money. That's all we ask."[22]

The Millers did have some income options of their own. Libby received an inheritance of $500 from her grandfather Peter Smith in September of 1843. Given their October 1843 marriage, that probably did not last very long. In the early 1850s, Charles sold "150 cords of seasoned wood... at nine shillings a cord delivered in Peterboro." It is not known if he cut any of it. By 1861, they owned a rental house in Peterboro, but did not want to keep it because Libby saw it as "a disgrace to the village." And at one point, "Col. C.D. Miller" owned the "Peterboro Hotel" on the Gerrit Smith Estate which had transformed into a "liquor house." According to an Oneida newspaper report in the spring of 1858, "Measures are being taken to stop the business... that will doubtless be successful." Gerrit did not want such a business near his house.[23]

In 1864, Gerrit gave the Millers some income producing property in Oswego. "The property I gave you," he said, "will, I am confident, yield you now $4 to 5,000 a year over + above the heavy taxes—+ it will yield an increasing sum.... I hope your income in 2 or 3 years will be $7 or 8,000." The agreement between them was that Gerrit would annually make up the difference between what the property provided and $8,000. Gerrit's business agent in Oswego, John B. Edwards, managed the Millers' property for them at no additional expense. In November of 1872, he informed them of impending tight economic times.

> "We shall probably have but little, if anything, from Oswego for some time. The next receipts from your property in this place will have to be applied to paying city taxes of this year.... There will also be a considerable renewable of Insurance not long hence."[24]

By the 1870s, their property was providing a substantial income, and actually met Gerrit's $8,000 expectation for the 1869-1870 year. For the year 1870-1871, Gerrit needed to pay the Millers $2,330 to make up the difference to meet their $8,000 yearly income; for 1871-1872 it cost him $3,857. In the last year of Gerrit's life, the Millers actually owed him $2,463 because their income was that much over $8,000.[25]

In sum, Gerrit graciously met the financial needs of the members of his family. He did appear at times to be reluctant to do so, but that was probably a defense against his constant concern of insolvency, combined with his desire to help the less fortunate. Even though he was very rich, because there was no insurance protection for investments, any financial difficulty could result in "panic" based recessions. An example of his reluctant, yet indulgent, attitude is revealed in his poem to his recently married daughter:

> "That Lillie's a lady + puts on grand airs
> Is proved by her buying two sumptuous chairs—
> The one costing thirty, the least twenty-five—
> Who else could spend so + still keep alive?
>
> Not to sanction her pride—but to relieve the distress
> She's brought on her purse by this great wickedness,
> I send her a present of just twenty Vs (fives)
> And wish her a new year of comfort and ease."[26]

He objected to "Lillie's" extravagance, but still paid the bill.

V

Early Residences

For the first two and one half years following their October 1843 marriage, Elizabeth and Charles lived in Cazenovia, just 10 miles west of Peterboro. Probably Charles' job at the bank there was an important reason for that choice. The house still stands, known as the "Truax House" after a family that owned it after the Millers left. Its current address is 15 Sullivan Street.

15 SULLIVAN STREET, CAZENOVIA: ELIZABETH AND CHARLES' FIRST HOME.
PHOTOGRAPH BY THE AUTHOR

Ann missed having Libby in Peterboro, and in standard mother fashion, made recommendations to her daughter. A servant, of course, would be necessary to perform such tasks as washing, ironing, cooking and taking care of the kitchen. And a proper chair for Libby and a "stand to hold your waiter" seemed necessary.

By March of 1845, Libby had "Mary" and "Elijah" working for her at the Cazenovia house. When she seemed to need help, Ann went to Cazenovia to stay for a few days. Also in March of 1845, Gerrit offered them living space in the Peterboro mansion because he had something special in mind for Charles.[1]

Due to the negative economic effects of the Panic of 1837, Gerrit and Ann were living at "The Grove" one mile south of Peterboro and Gerrit had released his business clerks, except for Caleb Calkins in Peterboro and John B. Edwards in Oswego. He wanted Charles to become his "additional clerk" at Peterboro, and to move into either the "Dr. Powers House" across the green from the Smith mansion, or to move into the empty mansion. Gerrit's offer included a number of attractive features.

He offered Charles an annual salary of $800, twice as much as he would pay to "some other person." He also offered to fill the ice house, provide new carpeting, and pay any building maintenance bills and all the taxes. Regarding the grounds, "the orchard, door yard, + cemetery will... furnish you... all the hay you will need." That is an interesting note. Yards were only mowed twice per year with a scythe, and the "produce" was used.

Gerrit's reasoning for this proposed move for the Millers was both personal—he and Ann wanted them to live closer—and business-related. He felt that because of Charles' connection to the Smith family, his interest in and commitment to the business would be high. Also, because Charles would someday be co-executor of Gerrit Smith's will, he should know as much as possible about the land-sales business. Gerrit recommended that Charles "close his employment in the Bank by the middle of April" so that he could start clerk duties by May first.[2]

Ann told Libby not to accept the offer just because her father had offered it, but only if they felt it was good choice for them. They hesitated on the offer for one year. In April of 1846, Charles resigned his position as cashier at the Madison County Bank in Cazenovia and Gerrit noted to a friend, "Charles and Elizabeth are preparing to move [to Peterboro]."[3]

THE SMITH MANSION. THE MILLERS LIVED HERE FROM APRIL 1846 TO 1850. THE MANSION, WHICH BURNED IN 1936, WAS VALUED AT $25,150 DURING THE MID-1800s. IT WOULD BE VALUED AT ABOUT $1,760,500 TODAY.

FROM THE AUTHOR'S COLLECTION

The Millers lived in the Smith mansion from late April of 1846 to the end of 1850. The census of that year lists their residence as having a value of $25,150 ($1,760,500 today)—certainly the large mansion. They moved into their own home across the Peterboro green in January of 1851. Gerrit gifted them with the house, the deed being recorded on January 3, 1851. The 1859 Peterboro map shows the house at the southwest corner of the green as being the "CD Miller Res."[4]

The summer and fall of 1852 saw renovations to the interior of their new residence. The heating facilities needed repair. "There is no partition between the two parlors—the chimney has been torn down up to the loft." And they were "sprucing up" the house with new carpet, curtains, furniture, and wallpaper. "I think," Libby said to her mother, "you will be delighted with the house when everything is in order—that will hardly be in less than

THE HOUSE ON THE PETERBORO GREEN. THE MILLERS MOVED HERE IN JANUARY OF 1851 AND PERFORMED MANY RENOVATIONS AND REPAIRS TO BRING THE HOUSE UP TO A STANDARD OF LIBBY'S LIKING.   *PHOTO BY THE AUTHOR*

a month." As part of her "news" for Ann in this letter, Libby mentioned connections with and facts about 27 other people.[5]

By the fall of 1853, Elizabeth and Charles were making plans for an extended stay in Washington, D.C. Gerrit had been elected to the U.S. Congress as an independent, and they were to attend to his needs there. Curiously, there is a very slim "paper trail" of their eight months there, except for Gerrit's formal participation in the halls of Congress. A few clues are to be found in a poem by Betsey Kelty, written to Libby:

> "My darling Lib—at thirty one
> You're fitting up for Washington.
> With Dad + Mom you're going down
> To see the laws done up quite brown....
> While you the household cares will guide
> With faithful Charlie at your side.
> And Willie romping, fat + gleesome
> Will keep the house from being lonesome."

Libby's job there was to revolve around "household cares." It appears that Ann and Charles returned to Peterboro, probably with Willie, Libby's three-year-old son.

The election of Gerrit Smith to Congress was astonishing—even to Gerrit himself. He received a plurality of votes among three candidates from District 23, which that covered Madison and Oswego Counties. His election was a superb political irony: he was never a member of any political party; he detested politics, did not campaign, and asked his constituents not to elect him. But they did! As his early biographer Frothingham put it,

> "Here was... an independent going where the party politician alone was regarded;... a servant and friend... going to the one place in American where... the arts of deception, invented in contempt and practiced with heartless cruelty, were prized...."

Gerrit was bound to be an out-of-place figure there.

> "The man of prayer is sent down to the metropolis of profanity; the free soul to the stronghold of slavery.... The people wondered;... editors smiled... sarcastically; the politicians derided; the high-minded rejoiced."[6]

Even though he did not want to go to Washington, he took the charge seriously. He purchased a house as his residence there, and had extensive alterations done to it. A cow stable was removed, the dining room enlarged, a bathroom added, and a carriage house constructed. He sent ahead a pair of his own horses, and purchased a "Fine Close Coach." A month before he departed Peterboro, he sent his personal servant, John Adams, to see to it that everything would be ready for his arrival in December.[7]

As his personal attendant there, Elizabeth was subjected to and knowledgeable about all the people and forces that impinged upon her father. She regularly wore the bloomer dress-reform outfit that she had designed, thereby making a bold public statement in a highly significant location for the blossoming women's rights movement. She met at their house, and likely conversed with, dinner guests Stephen A. Douglas, Charles Sumner, Salmon P. Chase, Joshua R. Giddings, Alexander H. Stephens, and many more legislative giants. Gerrit hosted two "cold water" dinners each week, serving 219 members of Congress, many of them southerners like Preston Brooks who were determined to support slavery.[8]

While in Washington, Gerrit and Elizabeth spent approximately $20,000 from the land sales business ($1.4 million today) in just eight months. Their time was that short because on August 7, 1854 Gerrit submitted his resignation from Congress. At that time, the U.S. Government was dominated by the "Slave Power," and Gerrit learned that his position as a reformer was insignificant. He knew that he could have more influence on the process of abolishing slavery by operating his successful business in Peterboro than by remaining in Washington.

By August 20, 1854, Elizabeth was back in her Peterboro home. She announced that "Catherine Foley is in my service from this date at $10.00 per week." Over the next three years, she hired "Katie," "Alice," "Mary Brown," and "Margaret Glen" at various times to perform "house cleaning" work. Charles kept a garden near the house in which he grew "large potatoes," while Libby worked at those domestic tasks that she enjoyed. When her daughter Anne was eight months old, Libby made "a cloak… of flannel" for her, and included samples of the pink lining and blue outer cover in her diary. When "Nannie" (Anne) was 1.5 years old, she went with her parents, and brothers Gat and Dudley, Jr. to Raritan Bay, NJ for six months. Willie stayed with the Smiths in Peterboro. Libby noted in her journal: "Sept. 9, 1857—We are prepared to leave for Raritan about the 10th of next month to spend several months. Gattie + Dudley will be in Mr. Weld's school." So they spent that time living away from Peterboro.[9]

The Millers lived in their Peterboro home on the corner of the village green for 18 years before moving to their final residence—Lochland on the shore of Seneca Lake near Geneva, NY in 1869. For a brief period in 1863, they considered Gerrit's offer of a residence in Oswego, but Elizabeth responded, "It seems better to me now not to settle permanently for some time." When that time came in 1869, their lifestyle would change dramatically. But in the meantime, Elizabeth and Charles would spend their days rearing children in Peterboro.[10]

VI

Children

Elizabeth and Charles had four children between 1845 and 1856, all of whom were reared in Peterboro. What follows about them here is not intended to be biographical, but rather a brief sketch of their lives.

Gerrit Smith Miller was born in the Millers' first home in Cazenovia on January 30, 1845. In early January, Ann suggested to her daughter that she "come home [to Peterboro] once more before you increase your cares. The sleighing is fine." Winter roads were not plowed then, so a horse-drawn sleigh was the means of travel. Ann wanted to coordinate her schedule with that of Libby so that "you will be likely to have the presence of some one of the old stock for several weeks to come."[1]

When "Gat," as they called him, was born, Ann was gleeful with optimism. "I shall live my young days over again with my grandchild." "Aunt M" wrote to Ann with glowing thoughts about the event.

"How happy you all must feel that the great event is over and that Dear Lizzie is so comfortable. Charles must have grown a foot since the 30th."[2]

But February 1845 offered some challenges. Ann hoped that "The Lord spare [Gat's] precious life," and that "the dear boy" would grow "whiter." It appears that he might have had a temporary problem with infant jaundice, a common condition that normally does not need medical treatment. Betsey Kelty expressed the family's concerns well.

"How much <u>more</u> I want to see you + the baby now, than I did a day ago.... I could but think... of the fear that glistened on your dear cheek for a moment."[3]

By the second week of March this crisis had passed, and Ann resumed her standard practice of giving advice.

"It is time, my dear, for you to stop giving soap and candy pills to the dear baby. It may be injurious to him.... I am afraid the soap pill irritates too much."

This pill was a mixture of potash and castile soap made from olive oil and sodium hydroxide, a caustic compound sometimes called lye, used today as a drain cleaner. The "pill" was coated with sugar ("candy"), and was administered in cases of constipation.[4]

By the end of May, Gat was doing well, but was 10 miles too far away from his grandmother. "How is my dear grandson? I want to see him," wrote Ann,

"more than anyone else I can think of. His sweet placid face was before my eyes so much yesterday, and today too. The Lord preserve him and make him a vessel unto honor... for the master's use."

I suspect that Libby did not see the situation that way.[5]

When Gat was a year old in the summer of 1846, he had some sort of mild ailment, and was well enough by December that his mother accepted Ann's invitation to join her in Philadelphia for the winter. "I dread leaving dear Gattie," wrote Libby, "but I know that I shall have a far more comfortable time without him, good as he is." When he was two years old, Sarah Grimké, an abolitionist friend of the Smith family, visited Elizabeth in Peterboro, and commented on her fine "domestic accomplishments," and of her superb "discipline both of yourself + the boy."[6]

Gat's formal education started at age six in 1851 at a school in Belleville, NJ operated by Gerrit's abolitionist friends Theodore and Angelina Weld. Gerrit and Ann's son Greene was also a student there at the same time. The school started in October, just two weeks after Ann had learned from Angelina that "they have had a good many cases of dysentery and some deaths about Belleville. It is well the children are not to go till 1st October. I should not wonder if the opening of the school should be deferred still later."

She then asked Libby to "keep an eye on dear Greene." Also attending this school in 1851 was a son of women's rights activist Elizabeth Cady Stanton, and a son of the abolitionist presidential candidate James G. Birney.

After dealing with Gat at his school for three weeks, Mr. Weld told Ann that "he would rather part with any boy than Gatty. He says he is the most straight forward manly boy in the school." Libby went there to visit the boys in mid-November.[7]

In 1860, Gat became a student at Epes Sargent Dixwell's Latin School in Boston, MA. There he became an avid sportsman involved in baseball and soccer, and is credited with organizing the first professional "football" (as it was called then) team. He was honored by being inducted into the National Soccer Hall of Fame in Oneonta, NY in 1993. Gat married Mr.

THE CAPTION FOR THIS NOV. 9, 1923 PHOTO READ:

"HONORING THE 'DADDY' OF AMERICAN FOOTBALL — (BOSTON) THE MISSES SUZAN AND MARTHA WIGGLESWORTH ARE PICTURED ABOVE, UNVEILING A TABLET TO THE MEMORY OF GERRIT SMITH MILLER, WHO ORGANIZED THE FIRST FOOTBALL TEAM IN AMERICA 52 YEARS AGO. THE MEMORIAL WAS UNVEILED AT THE NOBLE AND GREENOUGH SCHOOL AT DEDHAM, MASS...."

LIBBY'S SON, GERRIT SMITH MILLER (GAT), WAS A STUDENT AT EPES SARGENT DIXWELL'S LATIN SCHOOL IN BOSTON, MA. HE WAS ALSO CREDITED WITH ORGANIZING THE FIRST PROFESSIONAL SOCCER TEAM, AND WAS INDUCTED INTO THE NATIONAL SOCCER HALL OF FAME IN ONEONTA, NY IN 1993. INTERNATIONAL NEWSREEL PHOTO

Dixwell's daughter, Susan, on November 21, 1867 in Peterboro, and they lived in The Cottage Across the Brook on the Gerrit Smith Estate. The Cottage is currently owned by this author and his wife Dorothy H. Willsey, so I sit writing in Gat's living room.[8]

Gat entered Harvard College in 1865, but terminated his studies early and did not graduate. After an illustrious career in dairy farming, he was awarded an honorary Master of Arts degree from Harvard in 1924. His interest in dairy cows was stimulated during his time in Massachusetts when he saw a herd of high producing cows at Belmont. He and his younger brother Charles Dudley Miller II followed up by visiting Holland to study Holsteins, and in 1869, imported the first registered Holstein cattle into the United States. Gat's farm at Peterboro became well known for its success at breeding highly productive Holstein cows. He worked diligently at managing his dairy herd and keeping extensive records. When he was 25, his grandmother Ann, who lived only one quarter of a mile from his farm, commented, "Dear Gat is so busy on his farm that I seldom see him."[9]

There is very little information available on the young life of Elizabeth's second child, Charles Dudley Miller II. He attended the Welds' school with Gat in 1857 with the hope of taming what Libby called her "young barbarians." From September 1857 to May 1858, Elizabeth and Charles stayed in New York City near their boys while they were in school. Charles worked there "examining the writing books." Sarah Grimké, Angelina Weld's sister, was pleased that the Millers were "willing to entrust them to our care." Part of their schooling was called "moral training"—an effort to quell selfish impulses.

"Dud" was with Gat in Boston in the early 1860s. Both "boys" were well-liked by Mr. Dixwell. When Elizabeth Cady Stanton—"cousin Lib" as they called her—planned to meet with them in New York City, they did not show up at the appointed time. "Such is man," said Stanton, "even in embryo."[10]

During 1867-1868, Dud traveled in Europe and attended schools in England and Germany, learning to speak both French and German. In 1869 he worked as an employee of John B. Edwards, Gerrit Smith's business clerk in Oswego. He called himself a "real estate agent," and managed his mother's property there, making repairs and collecting rents. He sent Libby payments from her rental properties in Oswego.[11]

Dudley seems to have tried several occupations during his twenties. In 1871, he had sold his "Peterboro property" in order to set himself up in the lumber business in the vicinity of Otter Lake in the Adirondack Mountains. He employed over seventy people, and built a new sawmill in 1872. Then in 1873, he used a $6,000 loan from Gerrit Smith to become a partner in a stone quarry business. "Williams + Miller, Quarrymen" had a New York City office where he worked. He was still there one year after his initial investment, and had "improved the appearance and usefulness" of his rented room by the purchase of furniture. Tragically, Charles Dudley Miller II was involved in a streetcar accident in Syracuse on October 3, 1894. He died on October 7.[12]

Before the birth of William Fitzhugh Miller on September 21, 1850, Elizabeth had been having problems during her pregnancy. Her Quaker friend Sarah Grimké wrote, "How my spirit craves for thee a safe… and easy deliverance from the precious burden thou has been bearing. I rejoice in the belief that thou wilt… soon forget thy sorrows in the joy of a mother's love. I rejoice too in believing that angels will surround thy bed, and sustain thy fainting spirit."[13]

But Libby's "sorrows" regarding Willie would not end soon. For most of his short life he was plagued by illness. Exactly what it was is puzzling. Shortly before he died at age 26, Libby referred to him as being "pressed with some devil." Whether this "devil" was physical or psychological is unclear. It may have been both.[14]

For the first 10 years of his life, nothing abnormal is apparent. Betsey Kelty wrote a poem on his 10th birthday referring to his overactive behavior, some "naughty" things, and the need for "Will" to "mind" his mother. During the winter of 1861 while his parents were traveling in Europe, Willie stayed in Utica, perhaps with some of the Miller family who lived there. By this time, Willie had symptoms of some illness. Libby wrote to Gerrit from Paris, France, "I long to know what you have concluded to do with Willie.… I don't know but he is better off [at Utica] than in Peterboro." By the spring of 1863 his symptoms were clearer. "Poor Willie," wrote Libby in her journal, "was seized with inflammatory rheumatism from which he was a great sufferer for six weeks." And in the fall of 1863, "I took Willie to New York [City] to be treated for St. Vitus Dance." Known today as Sydenham chorea it involves rapid, uncoordinated jerking movements usually affecting the face, hands and feet. It is caused by a Streptococcus infection, and accompanies 20% to 30% of cases of rheumatic fever. In Willie's case, this affliction lasted for three months. During that time, Gerrit wrote:

> "God help little Willie! + free him from pain,
> And raise him to health + to vigor again:
> God bless little Willie! And make him to grow
> In patience + kindness + goodness also."[15]

Elizabeth took Willie to Boston for treatment during the summer of 1863. His symptoms included "inflammation of the pleura with a pulse of 114." Ann commented that "Lissie... looks worn out, thin + very little appetite. Charlie has taken care of Willie at night—poor little fellow. He is much emaciated [and] his breathing is very rapid." Obviously, Ann and Charles were there also. Later that summer, Ann advised Libby, "you must not return to your house this winter." Nannie (Libby's daughter Anne) was in Peterboro with Ann and Gerrit, and they were concerned about Willie's chances of surviving a Peterboro winter. By November, Willie's health had improved. "How full of joy we were last night at the news of Willie's wonderful improvement!"[16]

After the Miller family moved to Geneva in 1869, Willie developed an interest in raising chickens. The new home and his new endeavor seemed to settle his health symptoms for a while. Libby told her father, "Willie is working hard at his hen house." His breeding efforts must have succeeded, for he proudly bragged of a six-inch by eight-inch egg: "One of my Houdan pullets gave me a... token of her power as an egg producer." But by the fall of 1870, Libby had taken him to New York City for treatment by "Dr. Ressig." Ann noted, "I am glad you go down [to New York City] today with dear Will. It will be a satisfaction to you... even if it should do him no good." It appears that the family was losing faith in a favorable prognosis.[17]

Willie did have intervals of better health. In the summer of 1871, he was working at carpentry jobs at Lochland, cultivating his own orchard, and "is again at his studies." But by February of 1873 he had suffered some kind of "shock," and was away from home again for treatment. Writing to Libby, Ann was apprehensive. "I think, darling, you are the Greatest sufferer in this trial,... but God has given you great inward strength + you have the faculty of going 'into the stillness' when sorrow comes." And it appeared that "sorrow" was about to deepen soon.[18]

In the following year of 1874, Willie improved. Libby said of him, "I think no one on earth lies nearer to my heart than he when he is himself.... He is wonderfully genial + loveable when not pressed with some <u>devil</u>." But the "devil" returned, and Willie died on April 11, 1876.[19]

The fourth and last Miller child was Anne Fitzhugh Miller, born March 4, 1856 in Peterboro. Charles was present at her birth. Anne Fitzhugh Miller added the "e" to her first name. I will use that spelling in order to distinguish her from her grandmother Ann Carroll Fitzhugh Smith. After three boys, Libby was pleased to have a daughter "wrapped in her dear grandmother's flannel petticoat." Grandmother was also pleased. "How my heart is filled with joy," said Ann, "to hear of your safety and the birth of my dear little Nannie...." Notice the "my." Ann had had only one daughter that lived to adulthood.[20]

Elizabeth hired a series of women to help her care for Nannie. First came "Mrs. Hawley," followed by "Mrs. Elliot from Rochester [who] proved an inefficient woman, whom we were glad to get rid of at the end of four days. After that Mrs. Williams came in for a week, night + morning to dress + undress the baby." Later, in September, came "Julia." Having mainly domestic tasks herself, one wonders why Elizabeth needed constant help with the new baby.

Nannie had her picture taken on May 7 in Cazenovia. "We took her... to have her Daguerreotype taken.... Mr. Weld took two Abrotypes [sic] of Nannie—one in her father's arms + the other with me."

On June 10, Libby noted in her journal, "Nannie still thrives." Mom was well aware of the high death rate for infants, and probably kept her fingers crossed most of the time. At this time in mid-June, Nannie weighed 15 pounds. On October 17, Libby traveled to Geneva with Gat, Nannie, and the "nurse" Julia—probably by train. That was a major trip of 80 miles one way, taking probably four hours in the mid-1800s.

By Christmas time, Nannie had a couple of teeth and weighed well over 20 pounds. There was a trip "in her little sleigh" for Nannie and Willie on March 14 "to the mill pond where they are getting out ice for our ice house." Interestingly, such a detailed journal does not exist for any of Libby's other

ELIZABATH SMITH MILLER WITH HER FOURTH
CHILD, DAUGHTER ANNE FITZHUGH MILLER (NAN-
NIE), BORN MARCH 4, 1856 IN PETERBORO, N.Y.
FROM THE AUTHOR'S COLLECTION

children. It appears that there may have been more infatuation with the
female child than there was with the others.[21]

And the journal continues regarding Nannie at age one. "Our little darling nursed for the last time.... [Now] she spends an hour or more [eating]
a meal, + three meals a day have proved quite enough." That is, "enough"

for Mom, I think. A meal involved milk, bread, a fig, and a lot of "running about by the chairs."

At evening, "She goes to bed quite nicely—perfectly satisfied with her thumb + the blanket she is wrapped in. She... has become quite accomplished in French, [and in the morning] draws her finger very prettily over her lips + murmurs 'bonjour.'" Nannie was walking on her own by July 3, and loved going to the garden to pick "Bobbinies" (strawberries). "No one has been able to resist her pleadings for 'bobbinies.' Ever her Grandfather has left his papers to answer her...." Greene Smith's tutor, Edwin Morton, living at the time (1857) in the Smith mansion, "came over [to our house]... with a large cluster of very fine strawberries for Nannie," and gave her a long poem in celebration of her sweetness. Its last stanza:

"'O come, O come!' they sweetly cry,
O come + kiss us 'ere we die;
Come neath the morning's fragrant sky,
Or 'ere the day-torch flames ahigh,
Or 'ere the cruel gardner's nigh.
'O come, O come!' they sweetly cry—
The bobbinies, the bobbinies."[22]

At age two, Nannie was playing the "sweet little girl" role quite well— even on stage! She recited "Dickory Dickory" to an audience of 60, and liked it so much that she made a "second appearance" and would not stop speaking. She persisted in giving the audience ...

"Dickory Dickory dock <u>four times</u>!!! The applause affords her great delight. She claps too, with much spirit + to the amusement of all who see her."

Libby's visiting friend, Sam Wilkeson, wrote of Nannie's debut,

"the applause is ready for you darling, which shall mark with approval every act in the Drama of your life.... How you play the part of a woman—there are thousands to watch...."

And watch—and listen—they would when as an adult, she became active in the women's rights movement.[23]

Libby praised two-year-old Nannie as "a rosebud on a wild March morning"—like a sweet, calm spot in the storm of life. And she liked to get attention by feigning sleep in order to get kisses. Upon "waking" she would ask, "was it a rat?", and then softly murmur, "no, no!" As a birthday gift to her, Edwin Morton wrote another long poem on March 4, 1858 that spoke of Nannie's sweetness and her desire to be close to him. Its tenth and last stanza:

"And now, at times, the sweetest lips
Are pressing close to mine,
And golden curls are on my cheek
Worth many a golden mine.
That cry, that voice, those lips and curls,
O Darling they are thine
And yet to say again 'No! No!'
Does Nannie still incline."

But Libby's "rosebud" was not always perfect. At age four when Nannie had been "naughty," her mother would tell her that her "flag was down." To which Nannie replied, "Yes, and yours is sometimes down too mother."[24]

Nannie's schooling started early and was quite varied. Her mother's Sunday School class was first. Then on June 4, 1860, "Nannie commences school today. She goes to Margaret Woodbury in the session room of the Presbyterian Church." That winter, she was attending "Miss Fette's school." On a trip to Europe with her parents in 1867, she took lessons in German, arithmetic, and music at Miss Runtze's school in Dresden and lessons in riding and music at Dr. Hauslentner's school in Berlin. After the trip, Libby commented, "I rejoice in all she learned in Europe. It was acquired there with so much ease, + is now so useful to her."[25]

Nannie entered a school in New York City in early 1868 and, according to Libby, was "very diligent + will not neglect one of her studies." A year later in that city she was still in "Miss Nicolay's school" studying German and music, and in June of 1869 at Geneva she attended Mrs. Hopkins' school for music studies.

To continue with Nannie's "little girl" stage, she claimed at age four that she could not hear. Libby actually took her—along with Gat—to New

York City to consult with "Dr. Parker" about Nannie's deafness. He could find no physical cause for it, and told Libby "to drop a little 'glycerine' in her ear twice a week.... In a few days her deafness had disappeared!" I wonder if her "deafness" was restricted only to her mother.[26]

While the Millers traveled in Europe during 1861-1862, Nannie stayed with Gerrit and Ann in Peterboro. Gerrit was thrilled. He always did appreciate girls more than he did boys, probably because he felt no need to control them. He delighted in giving attention to Nannie. "She so delights in being upon my lap. In worship she sits upon my lap and joins in singing." She liked to sing the hymns "I Want To Be An Angel," and "Oh, Do Not Be Discouraged." "I never knew so lovely a child as she," said Gerrit. "She learns very fast." Although he claimed to be "very tired" because he missed "Lizzie's help," he did entertain Nannie's needs.

> "Dear Nannie came to me this morning for 3 cents more, another of her mother's weekly allowances to her. She is buying Christmas presents."[27]

At age five, Nannie had learned how to knit, "and is much pleased + very persevering." Gerrit approved and lavished praise on her. "Grandfather says I am the best little girl he ever knew." Libby worried that her father would encourage Nannie to get too good an impression of herself. While staying with him on her sixth birthday, she wrote a loving poem to her parents:

"Nannie Miller to Father and Mother in Italy"

> "Mamma, the rivulet hurries past our door,
> With ever hastening footsteps to the shore.
> Through lake and river speeding to the Sea
> To bear our native accents e'en to thee.
>
> Today Mamma they say that winter's gone
> And all the promise of the summer born.
> O dear Mamma, its richest boon will be
> That it shall bring your own dear self to me!...

Come soon then, Mother, to our last year's nest,
Where I so long have slept upon your breast.
Its maples green + simple vines + flowers,
Are dearer, sure, than all Italian bowers.

And there, you know, six years ago today
A stranger came from some far clime astray,
And from your boundless love so dear has grown
That every year she's more and more your own.

And, dear Mamma, somehow this day it seems,
In wakeful hours, or in my deepest dreams,
That over widening lands, + seas, + storms,
My childish heart to you + father warms."[28]

And just think—this heartfelt warmth and love so beautifully expressed by a six-year-old! And from what I have been able to discern, it would continue to be expressed toward her parents—and no one else—for the rest of her life.

During her pre-teen years, Nannie lived a very protected life in Peterboro. She cultivated a "garden by the bird house," developed interests in musical and artistic endeavors, and played the role of a sweet granddaughter. On her 12th birthday, she responded to Gerrit,

"Thank you for your very pretty lines to me on my birthday.... I bought a doll!... so you see you have me as your baby still, and you shall have me so as long as you like."[29]

After the Millers moved to Geneva in 1869, Nannie still lived a quiet existence without much further education. She became active in the woman suffrage movement in the late 1800s, and this book will delve much more into that subject later. At Lochland, she did become a skilled horsewoman, and continued her interest in music, flower gardening, and developed a personal interest in religious philosophy. Elizabeth did become concerned about Nannie's "sick headaches" as a teen, and commented that Nannie was "very delicate + we are uneasy about her." But such issues did not prevent her from living a long life. She died on March 1, 1912, one year after her mother's death, while on an "extended visit" to Boston. Her death certificate cites "natural causes, probably cirrhosis of liver." We can only speculate about what caused that.[30]

In sum, Charles and Elizabeth reared four children successfully, but did have to deal with the tragic early deaths of two of them. One final note of interest applies to all of them. Reacting to her father's generosity with money, Elizabeth wrote,

> "We have enough for the year. But I want all of the children to support themselves. If their pockets do not need it, their characters do. There is a wholesome order in it, which they cannot afford to lose.... I am not insensitive to your great kindness + generosity in saying you have enough for us all—but we don't want your old age to be burdened with our necessities. We should all put our shoulder to the plough."

She believed that "no one is <u>perfectly</u> developed who cannot, through head or hands, clothe + feed himself."[31]

One important question, especially in the context of nineteenth-century America, is: what role did religion play in establishing the ethos of a person as the foundation of the way they thought about and treated other people?

VII

Religion

Religion played a huge part in the history of nineteenth-century New York State, as well as in the lives of thousands of individuals. The revivals of the Second Great Awakening swept through central New York in the 1820s and 1830s, led by itinerant preachers like Charles Grandison Finney. He espoused a new brand of Christianity that rejected older Calvinist ideas of predestination, and focused on optimism and one's ability to change the course of his own life and that of society. This new world view ushered in the Reform Era that emphasized the restructuring of social life toward the achievement of equity among all persons based on natural, God-given rights. The empowerment of the individual that followed spawned the most important social movements in United States history—the abolition of slavery, and the advocacy of women's rights.

Born in 1822, Elizabeth Smith's early life was marinated in these issues not just by living in central New York, but also by being a part of a household that attracted into it nearly all of the leaders of both movements. Her father Gerrit Smith was, due to the combination of his liberal ideas, his money, and his philanthropy, the most powerful abolitionist in the country. And it was the abolition movement that spawned the women's rights movement. She sat at the Smith dinner table and listened to the radical ideas of escaped slave Frederick Douglass, Underground Railroad conductor Harriet Tubman, and women's rights crusader Elizabeth Cady Stanton. She saw firsthand the mutilated bodies of fugitive slaves, and talked directly with abused women like Harriet Powell. The forces that were pulling on Elizabeth Smith to embrace the religious values that led to these movements were enormous on both the personal and social levels. But she was also part of an era that encouraged people to think for themselves, to reject rigid and discriminatory perspectives, and to pursue their own peculiar self-actualization.

So it was probably predetermined that she would battle a high degree of dissonance in making decisions that related to religion. As a child, she was certainly guided by the religious orientations of her parents. Her mother Ann was a devout Christian for all of her life with Gerrit, and was the primary influence in the process of attracting him into that fold.

As a student at Hamilton College, Gerrit was quite secular. Three years after college when he and Ann married in January of 1822, he was still so. It was not until 1826 that he agreed to join the local Presbyterian Church in Peterboro. As Elizabeth matured, Gerrit did not badger her to be religious, but Ann did. Her letters read like sermons, full of warnings and potentially horrible consequences. The family held daily prayer sessions in their home, and attended worship services regularly. But as early as age 11, Elizabeth was skeptical about the value of religion. Rather than confront her parents about it, she generally kept silent.

While in Albany in February of 1836 with Gerrit for an operation on his painful hemorrhoid condition, Ann wrote to Elizabeth in Peterboro, "I wish you would tell me something of the exercises of your own heart as to religious things.... You know you do not <u>converse</u> freely with me on this subject. You must try to [speak and] write freely on it." Then came the warning.

"Search yourself my dearest and see that you do not rest on your own righteousness... but rest on the perfect righteousness of our blessed Jesus for salvation."

That is, Elizabeth's own thoughts and evaluations on the subject were not to be considered valid; she should instead simple-mindedly accept the "perfect" judgment of a mythical figure. Although it would take Elizabeth many years to resolve the dissonance she felt, she generally ignored such warnings.[1]

While she struggled with contradictory thoughts, Elizabeth wrote to her father, "You wished me to tell you the exercises of my heart on religious subjects. I have had some doubts about my hope, yet I have not given it up. I like secret prayer. I have been trying… this week to do unto others as I would they should do unto me. I am sorry that I did not resist the temptation of doing otherwise once or twice…." While she felt "doubt" about the value of religion on this social or group level, she did find some psychological value in it for herself in compensating for her feelings of grief over the recent loss of her sister Ann and her brother Fitzhugh. She felt certain that they had gone to heaven, and called it "the best resting place" for those she had loved.[2]

While Elizabeth's vacillating did not bother Gerrit much, it did bother Ann. Gerrit just babbled on in his letters about religious concerns:

"The Lord be with you my dear Nancy, + with my dear Libby—and may you both increase greatly in holiness + usefulness + happiness— and may we be preserved to see such things in the flesh + to thank him together for his mercies." God, of course, was always male—a power-based move by men then, as it is now.[3]

While Gerrit rambled on, Ann advised Libby, "I have many fears concerning your spiritual welfare…. Take care that you are not tempted to indulge in [worldly things]." "You must see to it, dear child, that… praise bestowed upon you… does not harm your soul." As Libby matured into her teens, Mom kept up the pressure. "How, my dear, is the health of your soul? Unless this is good, health of the body cannot make us happy. I wish you had always been more free with me on this point. Perhaps the fault is mine." And perhaps this insight on Ann's part was true. It could be that almost two decades of exposure to revivals combined with her mother's relentless harassment to do things her way had soured Libby's attitude toward religion. By the age of 19, she was coldly recording the dates and titles of sermons by local ministers, but nothing more.[4]

In 1843, two events helped shape Libby's orientation to religion. First, Gerrit led a group of local people out of the Peterboro Presbyterian Church. The break was motivated by the refusal of the church—and most other Christian denominations, as well—to oppose slavery. By this time, Gerrit was becoming more secular in his worldview, and was disgusted with powerful Christian denominations over their proslavery stand. As part of a new non-sectarian movement, he created his own Free Church of Peterboro, and invited any Christian to join it. This new institution was actually a political forum for the pursuit of antislavery goals by the newly formed Liberty Party. Gerrit was loudly criticized for mixing politics with religion, but because of his increasingly secular worldview, that did not bother him.

As Libby watched this defection take place, she must have deeply questioned the motives and goals of a brand of religion that did not support the inborn human rights—the "natural rights"—of all persons.

Second, in October of 1843, she married the very secular Charles Dudley Miller. Shortly after the marriage, Ann was preaching to Charlie, "My children, my heart longs after you with tears that Charlie may be 'born again' + that Lizzie may come under a fresh baptism of the Holy Ghost...." And in an interesting effort to twist Charlie's arm—or head!—Ann equated being a non-believer to being a slave. "Faith [provides] freedom from the iron bondage of unbelief. What an unspeakable liberty it is. They only are free who have it—all others are but slaves." Ann was mired in the Christian propaganda that thinking for oneself results in "iron bondage." She grieved over the fact that Libby had not fulfilled her wishes that she "enter the way of faith." Even Gerrit was distressed that Charles and Libby did not attend church.[5]

As the years passed, those soliciting Elizabeth's conversion did not let up. Writing to Charles and Libby, Ann encouraged, "the cultivation of your minds," and sent to them "a sermon of Mr. Finney's containing some reflections which may be of service to you both." Even friends who were not near Peterboro worried over Elizabeth's secular ideas. Sarah Grimké, one of the teachers of her children at the Belleville, NJ school, warned, "Oh Elizabeth! To know God, to feel his love pulsating in our hearts,... this is happiness.... [With acceptance of Him], the spirit will be better prepared... to drink with more delight at the fountain of eternal wisdom."[6]

And perhaps to influence Elizabeth's secularism even more, in the late 1840s Ann adopted an intense belief in Spiritualism, a system of belief that claimed that the dead could communicate with the living. Ann had séances during which she "spoke" with her dead children. Gerrit thought the practice to be silly, but tolerated Ann's belief, hoping that "you will soon outgrow this nonsense." Libby asked her cousin Elizabeth Cady Stanton, a clear thinker and respected social critic, what she thought of Spiritualism. She replied, "I am convinced that it is all humbug... [a] miserable piece of chicanery!"[7]

In spite of her growing secularism, even in middle age Libby did harbor some dissonance. At age 38 she agreed to teach Sunday School in Peterboro, and at 42 wrote a poem praising Gerrit's Free Church as being "true to God + true to man." But the intensity of belief that her mother tried to "cultivate" in her never developed. While on a trip to Europe in 1867, Libby witnessed 60,000 people worship "the chemise (undergarment) of the Virgin Mary" in Luxembourg and wondered,

> "How can there be progress in any direction when the world is so burdened with degrading superstition?"

And later in life when asked about her opinion regarding the truth of what is taught in the Bible, she said,

> "I who do not believe in its inspiration, cannot expect my views to be accepted by those who most reverently regard it as the Word of God."[8]

Given that Libby never did match up to her parents' desires for her on the religious front, what personal interests did she develop that made her feel good about the world and herself?

VIII

Personal Interests

Perhaps the major personal interest of Elizabeth involved the collective feelings of the entire Smith family—they loved being together. Visits by family members were occasions of high anticipation and elation. "We are always ready to greet you," wrote Ann to Libby. "Your comings are always fresh to us." She spoke of the "happiness" their visits brought, and of making "some little preparation" for them as a reward. And when the children were also present, that brought extra pleasure—"It is sweet to have them." Ann liked playing backgammon with them, and watching them play outside. If Elizabeth's family could not be present for a while, Ann cherished the privilege of looking at "the tin types" of them. When Gerrit was sick, family togetherness meant even more. Said Ann, "I write you now to beg you to come as soon as you can... to see us."[1]

The Smith "family" included house servants also. "Aunt" Betsey Kelty (Elizabeth Hebbard Kelty) filled that role for decades, and was treated lovingly. Libby said of her,

> "Such wisdom, love + gentleness
> Blessing all with their sweet influence
> Will leave a light behind them
> Which neither time nor sin can darken."

And again on Betsey's seventy-third birthday,

ELIZABETH HEBBARD KELTY, A HOUSE SERVANT WHO SERVED FOR DECADES IN LIBBY'S HOUSEHOLD, WAS LOVINGLY REFERRED TO AS "AUNT BETSEY." SHE WAS REGARDED AS FAMILY IN THE SMITH HOUSEHOLD, AND LIBBY SPOKE VERY PASSIONATELY ABOUT "AUNT BETTIE" ON SEVERAL DIFFERENT OCCASIONS. *FROM THE PETERBORO AREA HISTORICAL SOCIETY*

"What gift can I bring that is worthy of thee,
My dear Aunt Bettie at seventy-three?
Both tissue of silk and gold of the mine
Are paltry compared with such merits as thine."[2]

Even "Cousin Lib," Elizabeth Cady Stanton, was considered to be part of the family. As a teenager, she had spent summers with the Smiths in Peterboro, and warmly remembered those good times. Elizabeth Stanton and Elizabeth Miller called each other "Johnson" and "Julius" respectively. They adopted those nicknames from a comedy performance they had witnessed from the Christy Minstrels, and the names stuck with them over time. When Stanton had to cancel a pending visit to Peterboro, she bemoaned the last opportunity to enjoy "the quiet shades of Peterboro,... sentiment with Cousin [Ann], philosophy with Cousin Gerrit, and heroic life with Julius and Charles."[3]

Stanton nominated herself for a seat in the United States Congress in the fall of 1866. She did this in order to emphasize the irony of being eligible to run for office but not being eligible to vote. Libby invited her to come to Peterboro during that hectic fall to be with a confidant and maintain balance. Stanton liked the thought, saying that "a ride on horseback, a long walk with you [would] give more pleasure than a promenade in Broadway...."[4]

Smith family members valued and respected one another deeply. Mutual help was always available, and they worked out potential problems ahead of time in order to avoid family squabbles. In one such case Libby wrote to Gerrit to thank him for

"your kind regard for my wishes respecting [this issue]—it is very pleasant to know that... we need anticipate no difficulty with relatives."[5]

A very important way in which Smith family members expressed love for one another was through the writing of letters. With no telephones or email, this was their means of communication. The cost of sending a letter in the mid-nineteenth century varied between about six cents and 18 cents. Six cents today would equal about $4.20, so we should probably not complain about our postage rates. Ann once told her daughter to "stop eating candy—that will pay the postage."[6]

The letters they wrote were usually long and chatty, as if one were talking with someone in the living room. They contained lots of news about people, and described a day's events. Often there were "serial" additions in one letter. Started at 9:00AM, it would go on through the day with additions at 10:30, 12:15, 3:30, 6:00 and so on. The drive to "talk" with a loved one was constant, so the letter writing went on daily. When Libby was away from her Peterboro home from October 10 to 31, 1857, she wrote a total of twenty-three letters to family members. Ann referred to them as "lovely previous letters," and was "disappointed" when she did not receive them regularly. If Libby did not write to her often enough, Ann would issue a warning, "in the future I hope you will act contrary to nature in this matter."[7]

The process of writing letters was therapeutic. It relieved them of boredom and stress, and was an antidote to loneliness. As Ann put it, "I thought I would not write to you again 'till I reached Rochester, but I have such a longing to see you that I must write a little this evening by way of relief." And she did not mind making others feel some guilt. She told Libby, "I have not had a line from you [and] this is the third time I have written." When she did receive a "most satisfactory" letter, she reported, "Your letters create delightful little ripples in the even stream of our... life."[8]

Libby related to her parents very well, and, unlike her brother Greene, she was not perceived negatively by them. Although they did try to guide her into paths that they preferred, they did not try to force her into anything. When Libby was born, one of Gerrit's friends who had known him well in college said of his new fatherhood, "for a man of your peculiar feelings and ideas this circumstance will open new and endless sources of enjoyment." And so it did.[9]

Until his death in late 1874, Libby viewed her dad as a confidant, and they talked a lot. One subject that fascinated both of them was the beauty of nature. Gerrit saw a balance among diverse elements of nature that he used metaphorically in the development of his own brand of religion, and he loved the beauty of "Peterboro mornings." In December of 1860, a hoar frost covered everything, and inspired both of them to write about it. "But the woods!" exclaimed Elizabeth,

"Ah, what pen can describe them! Feathers of frost clung to every natural object—from the loftiest pine to the tiniest spear of grass.... The bliss of morning through such splendors filled the soul to over-flowing, +... seemed too intense for our earth bound spirit.... The poorest village maiden seemed a princess moving beneath the maples crystal arches. The unpainted house became a palace of enchantment."[10]

And on a summer evening as she walked home from a meeting,
> "The trees were all glorious in their summer robe of green
> And the setting sun with yellow light, gave beauty to the scene.
> While the birds, all joyous, their evening songs were singing,
> And the flowers, the sweet wild flowers, their fragrance flinging."[11]

Libby helped Gerrit however she could. She cared for and nursed him whenever he was in need; she gifted him often with his favorite items; she served him elegantly while they were in Washington, D.C.[12]

She was also an advisor to him. She counseled him about his less than proper table manners, made recommendations to him regarding his health practices, and even criticized his style of dress. Gerrit accepted her advice lovingly. Libby envied his ability to absorb criticism, saying, "I only wish I could be like you." Gerrit was so personally secure that others' criticisms and opinions of him simply bounced off. When their ideas did clash, the differences did not cause separation. Libby preferred a more extravagant lifestyle than did Gerrit, and he was not pleased with her orientation to religion, but they still were always mutually affectionate. In one cute exchange while she was living in the Smith mansion in late 1842, she asked him,

> "Can you, my dear Father, have fastenings of some kind put on the doors of my room? It would be a very great convenience when the room contains me." And, perhaps, Charles? I wonder if Gerrit provided the "fastenings."[13]

As Gerrit grew old into his seventies, he became infirm physically, and concerned about being "too old" to do what needed to be done. Elizabeth advised him to focus more on what he <u>was</u> still able to do. When he died on

December 28, 1874 in New York City, she was not with him, although she had been there just three weeks earlier. Libby was very saddened that she was not by his side at the end.[14]

Although Elizabeth had a close relationship with her father, that with her mother was even closer. They spent much more time together, both at home and away, than she spent with Gerrit. On the occasion of Libby's 51st birthday, Ann reminisced about decades of love. "I thank our Father in Heaven anew for the gift of such a child as you have been to me + your dear Father. Darling, you are a blessing to all who know you." She had said similar things on previous occasions.

"Thirty years ago this day I was filled with joy by being a mother. And now I am filled with joy that I am your mother."

When they were apart, they actually felt a kind of psychological pain.

"Tell dear Libby that she cannot think how much I feel the separation from her. I have not been so long from her in fifteen months. My absence from her makes me more sensible of my love to her."

When Libby was 33, Mom put her love into verse:
"This is for my own loved Lizzie
With heart + hands forever busy
Blessing our daily hours
Strewing bright fragrant flowers
all along our way.
How I rejoice to call her mine
To claim her thro' this brief earth time
My own heaven sent stay."[15]

Due to her dislike of Peterboro winters and her hypochondriacal view of her own health, Ann was away from home for two to three winter months each year. Libby usually went with her to comfort and care for her. "Dear Lissie!" exclaimed Ann. "Her attentions and tender care for me (so far above what I deserve) is overwhelming to me at times." Ann rightly felt that she was "free, my darling [Libby], to call on you for any service I may need." And that happened often. "Always weak and sick," said Libby, "[Mother] has not for years been able to say for an hour, 'I have no pain.'" Ann typically worried about everything: her health, Libby's time spent with her, the expense of treatment. Gerrit had written complaining about her high expenses, and that only made her situation worse. Ann's friend Nan Ledyard had read that letter and condemned Gerrit's "d...d lines to Mother."[16]

Libby's care for her mother was extensive even when they were not away from Peterboro. They lived across the village green from each other in the 1850s, so there could be daily contact. Ann noted,

> "I have been thinking, my precious child, how ever mindful you are of every wish of mine. I wonder how you can always remember with all your household + other cares."

And even after Elizabeth had moved to Geneva, she visited Peterboro whenever Ann needed her. After one such visit, Ann wanted her to "know how deeply I felt all your love + tenderness + watchful care...." One item that Ann appreciated as a part of her care and treatment was wine. I wonder how Gerrit felt about that.[17]

A big part of Libby's care and counsel of her mother involved the attempt to help her think positively. Ann's hypochondria, combined with her fear of growing old, reinforced her pessimism. And sometimes the advice between them flowed in both directions. When Libby was depressed, Ann noted a "sad letter" in which "you write bitter things against yourself...." Ann assured her that the "testimony of innumerable friends" should help her to feel better about herself. Most certainly they enjoyed a relationship that was mutually beneficial. After Ann died on March 6, 1875, the sense of loss felt by Libby was profound. Gerrit had died just three months earlier, and now Libby had this additional dose of grief to bear—which she did as she moved forward into the remaining 36 years of her life. But as she visited the old Peterboro homestead—the Smith family mansion—she observed,

> "I cannot realize that Mother is gone!... The house is lovely + peaceful as if both those precious ones were here, + it does not seem as if they had left us."[18]

The only other Smith family member was Elizabeth's younger brother Greene. Born in 1842 almost twenty years after Libby's birth, Greene was—in Gerrit's eyes—expected to become the heir to the family business. But as he grew past childhood, some incongruities appeared. He became an outdoorsman, and wanted nothing to do with the land sales business. Gerrit called him "my burden." Greene rejected religion, disliked formal education, and had no tendency toward philanthropy. Gerrit viewed him as a smudge on the Smith family reputation, and tried for many years to mold him to fit Gerrit's wishes. Greene rebelled and, when he could, left home. His relationship with Elizabeth was distant. They did not spend much time together, and, because of his chronic pain from fibromyalgia, he was often far from Peterboro seeking treatment. His hobbies of ornithology and shooting sports were both inordinately expensive, a fact that irritated Gerrit deeply. Elizabeth noted after Gerrit's death that Greene's habit of spending so much money had developed because he had never needed to learn the value of thrift.

When Greene died of tuberculosis in July of 1880 at age 38, that left Elizabeth as the only surviving member of the previously close and loving Smith family. Within her own family, the loving relationships she remembered from Peterboro did not develop, except for her relationship with her daughter Anne Fitzhugh Miller. Charles was a "distant lover," and her sons left Geneva to pursue occupations. Anne became Libby's loving companion—a sort of surrogate mother. They lived, played, and worked together at Lochland for the rest of Libby's life. To understand more about the adult Elizabeth, it will help to look at some of her personal traits.[19]

In the mid-nineteenth century, the proper role for a woman was in the domestic sphere, subservient to the dominant males in the household. So in nearly all of the writings about Elizabeth Smith Miller—even after she was long departed from Peterboro—she is referred to as "Gerrit Smith's daughter." When Gerrit referred to Elizabeth Cady Stanton as "Mrs. Stanton," she reproached him loudly for it, and asked if he would like to be called "G.S. Fitzhugh." In those days, a woman did not have an independent existence apart from some man.

To Libby's credit, she did always use her full name, and did not like to be referred to as "Mrs. Miller." She was a practical thinker with an open mind regarding different ideas and differences between people. She held little social bias, and was sensitive to the good qualities in any person, even if she disagreed with their convictions. Stanton's daughter Harriot Stanton Blatch described Libby as "calm... never perturbed. Her voice is rich and low, her speech always gentle.... She is so demure, so retiring, so shy, that it is difficult for a stranger to understand that underneath is rare insight, courage, and determination." And in public,

> "She talks very little; with strangers is almost silent. But she is a great listener; not one of those listeners whose minds wander from the point being discussed, but keenly following the conversation. Among intimates she is noted as quietly analyzing the problem we have been nibbling at and swooping down upon us from behind her knitting and in one brief sentence exposing the kernel of the whole question. I have seen her, in the gentlest manner, with a word take the wind out of a soaring philosopher."[20]

Physically, Libby was described as "a large, finely formed, beautiful woman, with raven hair, deep, dark [brown] eyes and an independent mind." One writer saw her "as fair as a picture, stepped living from the frame." She usually wore a plain dress adorned with only a Christmas rose, and perhaps a white lace shawl over her shoulders.[21]

Elizabeth was certainly blessed with every opportunity to live the glorified life of an aristocratic woman—but she did not. Her annual "income" was 16 times higher than the average of the time, and her regular social acquaintances were from the upper levels of intellectual and cultural life. Although she had been reared amid massive wealth, the ethos of her parents was oriented toward sharing their wealth with less fortunate people.

Her father's advice at the time of her marriage was to

> "Be careful, my beloved daughter, to get, + to keep out

LIBBY IN A PLAIN DRESS ADORNED WITH ONLY A CHRISTMAS ROSE, AND WHITE LACE SHAWL OVER HER SHOULDERS. *AUTHOR'S COLLECTION* of your heart all aristocracy. See to it that you sympathize with the masses, rather than with the conspicuous few.... Cast your lot with the despised and trodden down, and count as spurious [any idea] which stands aloof from them."

And from her mother, "I feel more and more the necessity of identifying ourselves with the poorest of the poor."[22]

Libby believed in education—especially for young women—as a means of upward social mobility. She supported educational scholarships, purchased books for people who could not afford them, and often gave money to poor people.

One of Elizabeth's traits noted by others was her "executive ability." Her home and yard were "well ordered" as she kept items organized and in place. A favorite saying was "Deliberate slowly—execute promptly." She handled efficiently a great deal of correspondence. As Elizabeth Cady Stanton noted,

"Every mail brings her letters from all classes, charitable institutions, prisons, Southern plantations, army posts, and the far-off prairies. To all these pleas for help she gives a listening ear. Her charities are varied and boundless, and her hospitalities to the poor as well as the rich, courteous and generous. The refinement and artistic taste of the Southern mother and the heroic virtues of the father are happily blended in their daughter. In her beautiful home on Seneca Lake, one is always sure to meet some of the most charming representatives of the progressive thought of our times."

And when she worked as a clerk for Gerrit, she organized items in the Land Office in such a logical way that when it was Ann's turn to be the clerk, she was certain that she could not keep the office as well as Libby had.[23]

Her days were very busy, with many contacts with other people. It is surprising that she claimed to be shy, and to "have a great dislike to exercising my conversational powers." Maybe so, but she did very well at it. People were impressed with her concise conversation. Her "work day" was usually so full of responsibilities that former Smith family tutor Edwin Morton was inspired to write a poem about it. In 1857 when Libby was 35, he wrote "The Busy Bee," which says in part:

"To count the honey you have stored
And gathered in the hive,
And fields of labor you've explored
For years full thirty five,
'Twere all in vain: no precious hoard
Can vie with that of Lizzie....
For industry, find some new word.
The bee's not half so busy."[24]

One issue that Libby found to be difficult to deal with was periodic bouts with depression. It was not debilitative, but it was important enough to her to be mentioned in correspondence. Her cousin Elizabeth Cady Stanton understood her concern. "I learn from your letter that your philosophy has not yet enabled you to combat that hydra-headed monster, 'the blues.'" She promised to teach Libby how to deal with it "when I visit Peterboro, which will be soon...."[25]

Libby loved the domestic role so much that it certainly had some influence in alleviating depressive feelings. One of the major projects of her personal life was the research and writing that went into the 1875 publication of her huge book of recipes and domestic instructions for the beginning housewife, In The Kitchen.

This book represents well what Elizabeth Smith Miller considered to be a major priority of her life—domestic elegance. And it highlights an interesting paradox. As we shall see, she recommends a clear division of labor between men and women based on assumed inherent differences, and also supports the notion that both sexes have equal rights.

Her book, published when she was 53 years old, was the culmination of decades of experience at making the domestic sphere of activity be an important portion of a well-balanced household and family lifestyle. A journalist reported that she "has the reputation of being the most accomplished housekeeper in the United States, having acquired the art by long experience in managing her father's hospitable mansion in Peterboro." The book manifested her desire to share that knowledge. "She was not content to reach only a circle of personal friends, but sought to share her expertise with a broader public...."[26]

The 592-page In The Kitchen was first published in 1875, and was reprinted in 1903. Libby dedicated the book to The Young Ladies' Saturday Morning Club of Boston. Organized in 1871 by poet and abolitionist Julia Ward Howe, the club sought to "promote culture and social intercourse" among young women—an emphasis not available in their traditional sewing clubs. They pursued "intelligent, useful and imaginative activities to enrich their lives" such as discussions on math, science, history, and the arts. A "cookery group" provided "culinary entertainment" that included "turkey muffins, hominy croquettes, and Quaker queer, a dish of creamed codfish that reportedly robbed Friday of all its terrors." A part of the club's scholarly pursuits were presentations by Mark Twain, Louis Brandeis, and William Lloyd Garrison. I suspect that it was the "cookery group" that attracted Libby's attention. It is not clear whether she ever participated in their activities.[27]

As a household guidebook, In The Kitchen was written because "some mothers... give their daughters no instruction in household matters, preferring that their time should be spent in study, recreation, and exercise in the open air." The implication here seems to be that such women are not well balanced. Libby says of the general intent of the book, "I have tried to make these directions... so clear that any young person of intelligence, who has never been in the kitchen and therefore has no 'judgment' to help her, can follow them to the letter and be rewarded with good [food]." Libby's cynicism here is clear. First, only women should be cooks; second, one who has not spent time in a kitchen has "no judgment." For Libby, the entire dining process from planning to clean up is to be supervised by "the lady," who, when things do not go well, experiences "a constant undercurrent of anxiety."[28]

Amusingly, the title of the book was a major issue prior to its publication. Several people suggested titles, indicating a fascination with the content and importance of Libby's project. Gerrit suggested "Choice Cookery," or "Light of the Kitchen," or "Kitchen King." Mr. Dixwell, Gat's father-in-law, offered "What, How Much, + How," or "From Hand to Mouth." Elizabeth Cady Stanton chimed in with "What Shall We Eat?," or "Artists in the Kitchen," or "Our Daily Bread," or "In The Kitchen." Someone suggested "Queen of the Kitchen," and when Gerrit proposed "A Cook Book," Libby called it a "hackneyed" idea because "all who see the publication <u>know</u> that it is <u>a book</u>."[29]

By October of 1874, Libby had selected <u>In The Kitchen</u> as the title, and wrote to her father to learn what he thought of it. She stated her rationale as follows:

> "<u>In The Kitchen</u> is short... + has the merit of being uncommon + just to the point. The receipts were all tried <u>in the kitchen</u>—they belong to <u>the kitchen</u>—I have been <u>in the kitchen</u> for the last two years making the book."

(Libby always used "receipt," an older, French-based spelling of recipe.) As Libby experimented with hundreds of recipes, Ann remarked, "We have had grand times with... Lizzie's testing of receipts." The results were shared among family members.[30]

The book was originally published by Lee and Shepherd Publishing Company, founded in 1862 in Boston. Edwin Morton, the former Smith family tutor, lived in Boston at that time and handled negotiations with the publisher for Elizabeth. He wrote, "Lee + Shepherd do not like your title for the book." So he suggested "Chosen and Rare Receipts in the Art of Cooking." Libby did not change the title. The book was ready for publication by October of 1874, and Libby was disappointed that it would not be printed until sometime in 1875 "because the publishers require three months, + I cannot send it to them until some time after I return home." She was in New York City with Ann for the winter. But Gerrit died on December 28th, and Ann on March 6, and that postponed the printing for another year.[31]

<u>In The Kitchen</u> opens with detailed instructions regarding the dinner table. The opening sentence reads: "No silent educator in the household has higher rank than <u>the table</u>." Its appearance signifies "neatness, order, and taste," or "carelessness and disorder." Libby emphasized that "an attractive, well-ordered table is an incentive to good manners, [whereas] an uninviting, disorderly table gives license to vulgar manners...." The tablecloth must be clean and well ironed with folds centered, dishes, glasses, and silverware clean and shining, with "knives, forks, and spoons... in line...." Plates and glassware must have no chips. Plates should be warmed, with tumblers and

napkins at the right, butter in ground glass dishes at the corners of the table, pitchers at the table corner with spouts pointed toward the center of the table, and salt cellars at each setting with a salt spoon nearby."[32]

The "three graces of the table," noted Libby, are "cleanliness, order, and taste." They create an atmosphere which contributes to the "highest development" of all family members and guests. Servants

> "should be as noiseless as possible. The voice of the servant should never be heard.... No reproof should be given a servant at table, and no instructions that can possibly be avoided.... No well-ordered house has noisy servants [for that would] stamp a house at once as belonging to the vulgar and uncultivated."

Poorly trained servants will produce "a constant undercurrent of anxiety" for the host, "for you have invited your friends to give them pleasure and not to tax their sympathy."[33]

Any meal should be leisurely. Doing things quickly to save time at the table is Libby's "chief objection, for time is the very thing we require at the table,—time to talk, laugh, and be merry." Clearing dishes from the table too soon would be "an unseemly introduction of work belonging to the pantry." But this is often sabotaged by "the gentleman of the house" who is more concerned with "dispatch than elegance." She considered the process of cleanup after a meal to be the responsibility of "the mother or daughter, thereby keeping the care and use of the kitchen under your own supervision."[34]

One area of work in which Libby was not quite as condescending to men being around the kitchen and the table was meat carving. That task certainly would require a person with "mechanical genius"—obviously not a woman! She even had her husband write the instructions. "One who is born," he said, "with no mechanical genius should never torment... or distract his family by attempting to carve; the office should be assumed by someone of the household more favored of the gods, who may, by daily practice and close attention, soon become... proficient in the art." And he said of the turkey, or whatever:

> "Let us carve him as a dish fit for the gods,
> Not hew him as a carcass fit for hounds."[35]

Libby recommended a variety of kitchen tools in the book. She listed seven items of wooden ware, 43 of tin ware, 21 of iron ware, and nine of stone ware—obviously a well-equipped kitchen. Wire baskets would be necessary for deep-fat cooking, and a raisin stoner for cleaning the seeds out of raisins. That is an interesting tool. Her reason for owning one was that "as it takes a long time to prepare fruit for a cake, a jar of stoned raisins... should always be in readiness.... Locke's 'Raisin Stoner' saves the tedious process of stoning raisins with a knife. They must first be stemmed, then, one by one, put through this ingenious little machine."[36]

LOCKE'S RAISIN STONER WAS USED FOR CLEANING THE SEEDS OUT OF RAISINS. LIBBY USED THIS MACHINE TO PREPARE FRUIT IN ADVANCE, WHICH SHE WOULD KEEP IN JARS, READY TO BE USED FOR BAKING. *FROM THE AUTHOR'S COLLECTION*

In order to store kitchen cleaning supplies, Libby recommended building "useful and ornamental" wooden boxes 30 inches long, 18 inches wide, and 24 inches deep. Perhaps those "mechanical" men could make them. The women would then line them with "chintz" (glazed, cotton printed cloth). Her effort here was to keep the kitchen uncluttered. And for economy, "use a... soap-saver for making suds in hot water for washing dishes," and be sure to save "drippings" from beef to be used in pastry, and from mutton for greasing tins.[37]

The most engaging part of In The Kitchen is the recipes themselves. The book contains approximately 1,300 recipes arranged in 27 categories, occupying 556 pages. Following each category are four or five blank pages "for additional receipts." Some recipes were contributed by others, and are so credited. And "most of these receipts have been tested by myself, and there is not one in which I have not full confidence." Of course, an unnamed ingredient in all recipes is the cook herself, or is it himself? For Libby, "there are natural cooks as well as natural musicians, and there is a charm in both that can never be reached by art." Poor art! "The delicate taste that decides whether there shall be a grain more of this or that in the seasoning... [is] like an exquisite ear... and graceful touch in music."[38]

One of Libby's most famous recipes was that for orange marmalade. She made loads of it, sold it, and used the profits to fund education for young women. For those readers who either love Libby, or just want to try to make orange marmalade, I include the entire recipe herein. I hope you can follow it!

ORANGE MARMALADE
Twelve pounds of fair-skinned sour oranges.
Twelve pounds of granulated sugar.
Wash the oranges and pare very thin as you would apples; put the peel in a preserving kettle with four quarts of cold water; cover and boil fast sixty minutes or until tender; drain and lay it away in a towel; throw away the water. When cold, the peel must be cut with scissors, into delicate shreds; for convenience' sake this may be done in the evening, reserving the last process for the next day.

Cut oranges in two, crosswise; put a strainer in the top of a pitcher placed in a two-quart bowl (a soup strainer with hook at the side saves the necessity of the pitcher). Squeeze the seeds and thin juice into the strainer; empty the pitcher into the bowl and set it aside. Have three quarts of cold water in a preserving kettle for the squeezed white skins; cover and boil them half an hour without stirring; drain and press in a colander, saving the water. Pound through the colander two and a quarter pounds of pulp from the white skins, taking a few at a time and throwing away the remainder. For the final process put the juice and water from the white skins in a four-gallon preserving kettle, boil fast for fifteen minutes, add the peel and pulp and boil five minutes, being careful that they do not adhere to the kettle; add the sugar and stir until it is dissolved, then boil as fast as possible for twenty-five minutes or until thick as desired. Try a spoonful on ice. Toward the last it requires close attention and frequent stirring. The tumblers (from twenty-four to twenty-six) may be filled and covered at once.

If sour oranges cannot be obtained, add the juice of several lemons.

Some recipes with a local flavor are included in the book. You may recognize the names involved in other sections of this biography:

Aunt Laura (Bosworth's) Breakfast Potatoes (217)
Viney's (Melvina Russell) Flannel Rolls (295)
Aunt Betsey (Kelty's) Little Hard Gingerbread (367)
Fossenvue Cakes (328)
Peterboro Cake (368)
Morrisville Candy (511)[39]

One conundrum for Libby involved the use of alcohol in cooking. Her own position was, "I do not reject wine nor, in many cases, brandy [in my receipts], but am happy to... give substitutes for them...." She consulted her temperance-oriented father on the issue, but found that his advice "does not help me." She was "troubled" about the recipes that required alcohol, but felt that "the book would be imperfect without them." She wondered if she might be increasing the sales of alcohol by suggesting its use in cooking. The advice from her mother was "that you had better let it go into your recipes. Those who have your book can use it or not according to their consciences." She did include alcohol use in a few of her recipes. And even though Gerrit opposed the growing of hops—a huge and profitable agricultural business in central New York in the 1800s—Libby did use it both in recipes that were flavored with beer, and in the making of three different types of yeast.[40]

In The Kitchen also provided recipes for a variety of non-food items. Libby instructed new homemakers on how to make hard water soft using lime or Borax; how to make soap from potash, grease, and lime; how to make good cooking fires from wood or coal; and how to make such necessities as cleaning fluid, disinfectant, glue, silver cleaner, furniture polish, waterproof boot-black, rust remover, cold cream, perfume, mosquito repellant, stain remover, and cough syrup. She even gave instructions on how to treat people who are sick, how to decorate your home, how to plan a good picnic, and how to preserve food.[41]

Although the interests and skills expressed throughout In The Kitchen are varied, they can all be described as domestic in nature, with nearly all of them taking place inside the house. Essentially, the book is an elaborate reinforcement and celebration of the "domestic sphere" as the proper place for women. It seems somewhat contradictory that an independent, well-educated, and human rights-oriented person would publish such a book almost three decades after the women's rights movement was launched in Seneca Falls, NY by her own cousin.

But we must remember that widespread prejudice against the social and economic advancement of women was more intense at that time than prejudice against African Americans. Black male suffrage legislation succeeded in 1870, but in spite of vigorous work by women, they would wait another five decades before men recognized the fact that they had the same right. In The Kitchen fit well the tenor of the times, and Libby rationalized the book brilliantly:

> "We must rejoice... that house-work is more healthful than fancy work; that making beds, sweeping, and dusting give strength, and that kneading bread, making biscuits, and canning fruit 'brush the cobwebs from our brains.'"[42]

A last look at Libby's personal interests will cover a variety of things she liked to do. For games, she enjoyed backgammon, and a card game similar to bridge called whist. She also enjoyed playing a guitar. She loved nature in the wild, and growing flowers in her yard—"especially mignonette" and Christmas rose. Inside the house, she grew ivies.[43]

A regular daily task for Elizabeth as early as age 16 is what I call "house management." She kept detailed lists of family expenses, items purchased, wages paid, prices paid, and distribution of products from the larder. Examining every detail of these lists gives one a view of their lifestyle. I will present here what I believe to be a representative sample from her "Day Book" records. An impressive feature of this "bookkeeping" process involves the level of commitment and the amount of time required to do it.

At the aggregate level is an accounting of funds transferred from the "Land Office" (business) account to the "House" for purchase of items needed for family life. These transfers are noted on a monthly basis. Then, at the household level, are long lists of hundreds of items and prices paid. A partial list of non-food items:

2 needles	1 porcelain kettle
6 plates	1 bath brick
2 candlesticks	5½ gal sperm oil
37 lbs candles	1 tin dipper
1 seive	2 stone jars
5¾ yds toweling	2 brooms
2 table cloths	2 iron spoons
2½ lbs soap	2 tin basins
1 brush	1 hammer
1 knife	2 hanks yarn

A survey of these items indicates some that are necessities, and some that are not. A poor family, for instance, would probably not be purchasing a porcelain kettle, candlesticks, or tablecloths.

A partial list of food items includes:

raisins	apples
blackberries	2 boxes cloves
dried cherries	1 doz lemons
2 gal syrup	1 pt. cream
10 lbs coffee	2 chickens
40 lbs sugar	4 squashes

1 bushel plums	almonds
4 doz eggs	melons
1 peck peaches	dried currants
1 bushel pears	1 box salt
4 lbs soda crackers	2 loaves bread

These partial lists represent items purchased over a two-month period only. The full list contains approximately fifty items, many of which are luxuries like cloves, syrup, and dried cherries. A few more examples of non-food items are "calico (cotton cloth from India), indigo (blue dye), flat iron, dish pan with handles, 4 gal. oil can with spout, 6 handkerchiefs, clothes brush, Christmas presents for 28 persons." These are certainly not necessities for survival. Libby even did such bookkeeping when she was attending school in Philadelphia.[44]

Although Peterboro did have over 30 active businesses operating in the mid-1800s, Libby could not have made all of her purchases there. She made shopping trips to Cazenovia, Hamilton, Syracuse, and Rome, and bought harder to find items on her frequent travels (as we shall see in the next chapter) to Albany, Boston, New York City, or Philadelphia. As part of her records, she even kept a list of her Sunday School students when she was 18 years old:

"Members of my S.S. Class Peterboro '41
Laba Lloyd -11 years old
Hannah H. Robbins - 9 years old
Ellen Dana - 9 years old
Luretta Harvey - 9 years old
Emily Barker"

She also enjoyed sewing and, of course, cooking. One list for May of 1854 shows 18 entries for the purchase of items used in sewing, and there are many other such lists. She made dresses for herself, shirts for Gat, and probably clothing for all family members. Her cooking skills are well documented in In The Kitchen, and she also taught cooking classes for young women (of course), and made special Christmas candies for local residents.[45]

Learning different languages also interested Elizabeth. She took lessons in French and German, and became proficient at speaking and writing French.

Some journal entries and letters to her mother are written in French. Writing was also a minor passion for her. Letters, of course, were written daily, and were often several pages long. She wrote poems, as is evident in the Smith family Verse Book, and she kept a list of "subjects for compositions" that she intended to write someday. That list included "The Laplander," "Liberians," "Indian Rubber," "Looking-glass," and 'Travelling." She even compiled an annual calendar that she called "Chimes Calendar." It was referred to by a journalist as "the most useful and amusing calendar ever published. [It] is printed in brown ink, on extra fine paper, the whole mounted on a finely lithographed card representing 'Harebells' colored true to nature." Harebell is a blue flowered herb. In the calendar, Libby included recipes, riddles, health hints, sewing instructions, poetry, and other notes of interest.[46]

An interesting feature of Elizabeth's life is the frequency of travel. As an urbane and refined person, she enjoyed getting away from Peterboro periodically, and the catalog of her travels presents a new chapter.

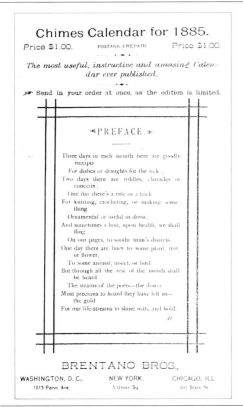

LIBBY'S "CHIMES CALENDAR." IT WAS REFERRED TO BY A JOURNALIST AS "THE MOST USEFUL AND AMUSING CALENDAR EVER PUBLISHED. [IT] IS PRINTED IN BROWN INK, ON EXTRA FINE PAPER, THE WHOLE MOUNTED ON A FINELY LITHOGRAPHED CARD REPRESENTING 'HAREBELLS' COLORED TRUE TO NATURE." HAREBELL IS A BLUE FLOWERED HERB. IN THE CALENDAR, LIBBY INCLUDED RECIPES, RIDDLES, HEALTH HINTS, SEWING INSTRUCTIONS, POETRY, AND OTHER NOTES OF INTEREST.

FROM THE GENEVA HISTORICAL SOCIETY

IX

Travel

During the mid-nineteenth century, traveling anywhere in the United States was a difficult and time-consuming process. And in wintertime where snow was common, it was nearly impossible because roads were not plowed. Even small villages like Peterboro were nearly self-sufficient. It was not unusual for a person to live an entire life within a few miles of their place of birth. A "trip" of 10 miles—say, from Peterboro to Cazenovia—was a day-long event, and if it rained, a wet and muddy affair. Gerrit wrote of his shoes being ruined when he had to get out of the carriage and help push it out of the mud.

This makes the frequency of Elizabeth Smith Miller's travel a source of amazement. During the period from 1840 to 1874—a total of 408 months—she was away from home for 104 of them. She spent one quarter of that 30-year period "on the road." The two major modes of travel were horse and carriage, or by train—"the cars," as they called it. And the expense of travel kept most people home. An October 1857 trip from Peterboro to Albany and back cost Libby $22.61. That cost adjusted for today would be over $1,500! When Libby and Ann traveled from Peterboro to Rochester in August of 1841, the process went as follows: a "buggy ride" from Peterboro to Wampsville—2 hours; "the cars" from Wampsville to Syracuse—1 hour; a canal boat from Syracuse to Oswego—4 hours; a ship, the "United States," on Lake Ontario from Oswego to Rochester—8 hours; a 15 hour trip! Today, that would be a two-hour trip on the New York State Thruway. Libby would be shocked.[1]

It is probably fortunate for Elizabeth's health—mental and physical—that she liked to travel. She went to New York City often, and wrote to Gerrit once while there in February,

> "The weather is charming! The streets clean + beautiful + the air soft + spring-like. How pleasant it would be were this our Winter home. For, although we enjoy the <u>visit</u>, there is not the <u>settled</u> feeling which would add so much to our pleasure."

But that pleasure was often limited. Most of Libby's trips within the United States—80% of them—were taken in an effort to improve her mother's health.[2]

Ann always seemed to be sick—or at least she thought she was. She called her hypochondriacal state of mind "being comfortably sick." She liked to get out of Peterboro for the winter, and usually went, with Libby as her attendant, to New York City. They stayed with "cousin Ellen" at 133 East 12th Street. While there, Ann tried a variety of "cures" including "movement cure," "water cure," and visits to a chiropractor. Of course, no treatment worked well, at least until April when the snow melted in Peterboro. While in New York, Ann and Libby did a lot of visiting of friends, attending entertainment shows—especially opera—and shopping at upscale stores. They often wrote to Gerrit, who was, of course, still in Peterboro, to send them more money. He always obliged.

Libby also traveled to other places across the country. On an extended trip to the Boston area in the fall of 1871, she and Ann stayed with Edwin Morton. The highlights of that trip included visits to Nantucket and Plymouth, and the chance to meet Franklin Benjamin Sanborn. Morton had been a tutor for Greene Smith in Peterboro, and his roommate while he studied at Harvard in earlier years was Sanborn. Sanborn was also one of the "Secret Six," a group of radical abolitionists who supported the activities of John Brown. On the windy, snowy day of February 23, 1858, Sanborn walked with Gerrit Smith around the grounds of Smith's Peterboro mansion while John Brown waited inside to hear their decision regarding the funding of his planned raid on Harpers Ferry, VA. They did decide to provide the money to support Brown's raid—the very act that ignited the Civil War. Elizabeth must have had a delightful conversation with him.[3]

Travel to other places outside of New York State included visits with the Fortens in Philadelphia several times, a trip to Chicago in 1868 to visit Greene and Bessie, visits with Ann's relatives in Hagerstown, MD, and the nearly year-long stay in Washington, D.C. in 1854.[4]

The major trip that provided an exclamation point for the Millers' lives was their December 1861-June 1862 European vacation with Libby's mother and brother. Thinking about her pending "trip to Paris," Ann wrote to Gerrit in October of 1861, "I could go beautifully with Charles and Lissie, but I could not take them from you." Yet she did. Libby and Charles left the younger children with Gerrit in Peterboro. Where Gat and Dud stayed is not clear. Gerrit's letters from Peterboro during the trip gushed with pride over his grandchildren. Elizabeth, Charles, and Ann planned to meet Greene in Lyon, France and have him join them for the trip. Greene had been in France for a few months attending school.[5]

From Peterboro, they traveled to Boston in late November, staying at the Parker House Hotel which had opened in 1855, and was recognized as one of Boston's finest. On their departure, Gerrit wrote them a farewell poem:

> "Goodbye, Goodbye my precious four;
> And as you journey Europe o'er,
> I'll work to meet your drafts on me
> And feel your joy'll my payment be."

It must have been comforting to them to know that there was enough money available for them to do anything they wished to do.[6]

They sailed from Boston at 2 p.m. on November 30, 1861, and were to arrive in Ireland on December 15. Ann reported, "I feel... sick nearly all the time, + rarely eat without an effort...." They docked at Queenstown, a port on the south shore of County Cork, Ireland at 7:00AM on December 15, and left for Liverpool, England at 10:00AM the next morning.

After a two-week stay in London, they sailed for France, staying in the vicinity of Paris for about one month. They met Greene in Lyon in mid-January of 1862, and then set out to visit the rest of Europe. Their journey covering February to June was divided into roughly two-week segments as follows:

Early February – Naples and Genoa, Italy
Late February – Rome and Florence, Italy
Early March – Florence, and back to Rome
Late March – Dresden, Berlin, and Hamburg, Germany
Early April – Paris, France
Late April – Zurich and Lucerne, Switzerland
Early May – Paris, France
Late May – London, England and Glasgow, Scotland
Early June – Glasgow and London[7]

That was a marvelously long and expensive trip, with plenty of recreational time at each venue. Early in the journey—I believe in France—they hired a guide. Louis Coudray accompanied them to each venue, making all the arrangements for hotels and travel. With some humor, Charles described the roles that each of them played during the trip. "Gen. A.C. Smith in command; Aid de Camp is E.S. Miller; paymaster is C.D. Miller; Greene Smith as drillmaster."[8]

A few highlights of the trip are worth noting. Not all of them were enjoyable. Their moves between cities in Italy sometimes took place on "disgustingly filthy little steamer[s]." At one point "it was very hard for us to make up our minds to go on the sea again after so much suffering from sea sickness." On a lighter note, they enjoyed an opera in Naples, and were impressed by the new carcel lamps used for lighting. The carcel lamp used a pump to move oil to the wick to provide efficient lighting. But while there, Greene experienced "terrible pain" from a toothache, and had to have it removed. Greene spent much of his time and Gerrit's money buying bird skins at city markets to add to his Peterboro-based bird collection.[9]

In Rome, they visited the Colosseum, the Pantheon, and St. Peter's Basilica. In Pisa they "climbed to the very top of the leaning tower," and in Florence enjoyed sightseeing among the art treasures. In Prague they experienced culture shock as they watched "women labor with the men—in the field, the woods, on the railroad, + even on the scaffolding of houses in mason work! Yesterday we passed a man + woman riding in a cart... the woman driving, whip in hand!" And that was Libby doing the writing.[10]

In Hamburg, Germany, they met King William I who "politely returned" their bows of respect. Libby asked Gerrit, "Do you think we can ever be contented in Peterboro again after reveling in the attentions of European Royalty?" In Strasbourg, France, Libby liked the "delightful music," and in Zurich, the "beautiful scenery." She did become ill in both Lucerne and London, but managed to continue with the trip.[11]

Near the end of their six-month journey, they stopped again in Paris, and Ann splurged. "Mother is launching out in great style," wrote Libby. "Two beautiful dresses + a pretty dove colored silk hat!... a lilac plaid silk, with pin + sleeve buttons of the charming Roman gold." And at dinner, she had "salmon, beef, macaroni, new potatoes + strawberries." Or were they bobbinies? Gerrit annotated this letter from Libby, "My dear wife supposed I would be pained if she spent money as freely as she wished!!!" He was not.[12]

As their trip ended, Libby wrote to her father, "Our trip has been charming. You think we will have a great deal to tell. Mother will no doubt, but telling is not my forte, either in the tabernacle or the family circle." As acquaintances always said of her, she was a quiet person.

Elizabeth did make one more extended stay in Europe from late November of 1866 to late November of 1868. This time she was accompanied by Charles, Anne Fitzhugh Miller, and Charles Dudley Miller II—that is, her husband and two of her children. They lived in Berlin and Dresden from November 1866 until September 1868, and in Switzerland and France for October and November of 1868. Strangely, there is little evidence of why they went and what they did there. Six months after their return, their lives were to change dramatically.[13]

X

Lochland

Elizabeth's desires for elegant living and proximity to an urban area were never met in dear old Peterboro. Her home there at the southwest corner of the village green was spacious and accommodated all of her family's practical needs, but did not meet "the standards of a King and Queen," as Gerrit would say. And although she enjoyed being near her parents, she could not completely assert her own independence in the shadow of the Gerrit Smith Estate mansion.

On their return from their two-year sojourn in Europe in late 1868, Elizabeth and Charles were hoping to develop a more elegant lifestyle than was available in the rural and isolated Peterboro, and, on the horizon loomed an amazing opportunity that must have seemed to be a mirage.

In the spring of 1865, Libby's brother Greene was discharged from the army after having served for a brief but traumatic time. He had been in the front line at the Battle of the Crater near Petersburg, VA on July 30, 1864. Although he survived uninjured, he witnessed many hundreds of deaths. Then, he was wounded in a subsequent battle. On returning home, his desire was to become a small-scale farmer in a location removed from Peterboro and the constant badgering of his father.

Greene and his new wife Bessie had examined "The Stone Place" on the western shore of Seneca Lake near Geneva, and had asked Gerrit to buy it for them. At first, Gerrit refused to do so, but he eventually did purchase it, and by June of 1865 Greene and Bessie were living there.[1]

As Greene settled in and relaxed, he gave his new home a name: "Lochland." The word is of Scottish origin, and refers to enjoyment of the beauties of the natural world. Greene wrote to his mother, "This is my first letter from this place to you. How do you like the name I have given it?" Gerrit gave him $1,000 to set up as a farmer. He bought tools, some hens, one cow, and hired Noah Frister to work for him at $32.00 per month. Within two years he was also raising deer on the sixty-four acre property.[2]

By mid-1868, Greene was experiencing the severe pain of fibromyalgia, and searching for help from both a skilled physician and a warmer climate. The physician he found in Chicago, and the warmer climate in Florida, so he spent the rest of his short life shuttling between Homosassa, FL, Chicago, IL, and Peterboro. Why Peterboro? Because after he eventually sold Lochland in later years, he needed a summer home near his bird collection in The Birdhouse at Peterboro. After his parents died one after another in 1874 and 1875, he and Bessie lived in the family mansion during summer months.

Greene advertised Lochland for sale in several newspapers from October of 1868 to May of 1869. His asking price was $35,000. When it did not sell quickly, he attempted renting it. In their search for an escape from Peterboro, the Millers had visited Greene at Lochland, and also examined the "Bunner House" in Oswego. Because she considered Lochland to be too expensive to purchase and too extravagant to maintain, Libby made tentative plans for renovations to the Bunner House. Then, in a surprise move, Gerrit purchased Lochland from Greene and gave it to Libby![3]

Elizabeth and Charles had been in New York City for the six months prior to June 1869. They returned to Peterboro on June 27, and "the next day Charlie + I went to Clifton Springs to see Father + Mother (Ann was there for health treatment).... Father had purchased Greene's place in Geneva + wished us to occupy it. We were quite opposed to doing so, as we felt it entirely beyond our means to live in so large a place, but Father was so very anxious that we consented to try.... The result was that July 5th we arrived in Geneva bag + baggage.... Soon after, Father sent us a Deed of the place!"[4]

Regarding the deed, Gerrit wrote to Libby, "I had intended to have Greene + Bessie's deed [transferred] to me, + then (when I should find you and Chs contented with the farm for a home) I to convey it to you. As I do not any longer doubt that you will both be contented with a home that should content a King + Queen, I have them make the deed directly to you. I send it herewith. I send also the policy of insurance."[5]

Elizabeth wrote in her grateful reply to Gerrit, "Yesterday came the deed for this beautiful home. We thank you most heartily. It is indeed, a magnificent gift—really fit for a King and Queen, as you say. We hope to make it a happy home for ourselves, our children, + our dear Father + Mother." Then she added, "We have written Dudley to bring three heifers from Deutschland." Charles Dudley Miller II (Dudley) and Gerrit Smith Miller were in the process of purchasing and importing the first registered Holstein cattle in the United States, and three of them were evidently headed for Lochland. After moving in, the Millers paid Greene and Bessie "about $2,000" for furniture that they had left in the house.[6]

An interesting observation is that after her arrival at Lochland, Elizabeth's desire for foreign travel vanished. She did still accompany her mother for extended stays in New York City in 1870, 1873, and 1874, but never again traveled to Europe. Perhaps her craving for elegant living was satisfied at Lochland.

Their lifestyle there became one of "quiet refinement," but not before they settled some financial concerns. In a mournful letter to Gerrit just three months after they moved in, Elizabeth gave the details of what she feared was a path to bankruptcy. She wrote: "You know how fearful we were in taking this place, that we would not be able to keep it. So confident were we that our means were not equal to so great an end that we decided we could not come here. But it seemed a hard, thankless thing to say to you in return for so superb a gift, + we compromised by saying we would try.... We find it just as we feared." She then detailed a list of expenses that made it impossible for them to live there. "What shall be done? I cannot consent to be a burden on your hands.... This is a magnificent place, but the owner should have an income of $15,000." Their income was $8,000. By late October, their financial woes had been cured by "dfts" (checks) from Gerrit, and the Millers were moving ahead with plans for their future at Lochland. "By February," said Libby, "we hope to be in 'easy circumstances.'" Some of their own income-producing property in Oswego was also helping.[7]

LOCHLAND WAS PURCHASED BY GERRIT SMITH FOR LIBBY'S BROTHER GREENE SMITH, A CIVIL WAR VETERAN. IT WAS ONCE REFERRED TO AS "THE STONE PLACE", BUT UPON ACQUIRING THE HOUSE, GREENE DUBBED IT "LOCHLAND", A SCOTTISH WORD THAT REFERS TO THE BEAUTIES OF THE NATURAL WORLD. EVENTUALLY, LOCHLAND WAS SOLD BACK TO GERRIT SMITH. GERRIT THEN OFFERED THE PROPERTY TO LIBBY AND CHARLES.

COURTESY OF THE GENEVA HISTORICAL SOCIETY

The physical beauty of Lochland was striking. A journalist described it as "an ideal residence, surrounded by a deep and lofty piazza, with spacious grounds sloping down to the lake, of which the broad windows command a noble view." Libby's gardens produced a profusion of "heliotrope, 'Christmas roses,' and large heads of mignonette...." Libby described

"a glorious morning. When I looked out, the shadow of the house lay on the lawn—then came the woods, the beautiful lake + the early morning light in the sky beyond.... Here comes the sun, perfectly magnificent! And now the lake begins to reflect its light, + beautiful shades of rose, green + blue lie on its surface; and now there is a golden path across the lake!"

There were fruit trees in the yard, and the huge porch was adorned with beautiful wisteria blossoms. One daylily garden in the shape of a horseshoe honored Charles' love of horses.[8]

THE PIAZZA AT LOCHLAND. EVEN THOUGH LIBBY WAS RELUCTANT TO ACCEPT HER FATHER'S GIFT, THE LOCHLAND PROPERTY, SHE VERY QUICKLY FELL IN LOVE WITH THE HOME. SHE WROTE HER FATHER THAT HIS GIFT WAS "FIT FOR A KING AND A QUEEN."

A JOURNALIST DESCRIBED IT AS AN IDEAL RESIDENCE SURROUNDED BY A DEEP AND LOFTY PIAZZA. THE GROUNDS SLOPED DOWN TO THE LAKE AND THE HOUSE, ADORNED WITH BROAD WINDOWS ALLOWED FOR A "NOBLE" VIEW.

COURTESY OF THE GENEVA HISTORICAL SOCIETY

THE PARLOR AT LOCHLAND. *COURTESY OF THE GENEVA HISTORICAL SOCIETY*

At various times in the 1870s, the Millers opposed the building of a railroad across their property, and the establishment of a cemetery nearby, but neither happened. In 1874, they received a gift of $5,000 from Gerrit for making renovations to the house. She reported to him that "our work is coming on well.... The improvements are wonderful!!" One of the changes was the addition of new double five-foot doors inside. Before they were finished, Libby asked apologetically for an additional $2,000, saying to Gerrit, "I am... very sorry that we require so much." They were so content at Lochland that when Bessie offered them the Peterboro mansion after Greene had died, they turned it down. "I must thank you," replied Libby,

"for your beautiful + generous offer of the dear old homestead!... But I see no reason for leaving Geneva." Lochland was just one-half mile from the city of Geneva, and Libby saw in Peterboro "too great an isolation."[9]

The Millers' elegant lifestyle at Lochland was supported by several factors. Certainly Gerrit's wealth was one. Another was the presence of servants. "We have a lovely home," wrote Libby, "beautiful + comfortable, + good loving servants ready to do everything for us." They prepared meals, cleaned the house, attended to the needs of guests, and maintained the grounds. Margaret Brilton and Georgie were two of them, but most were never named in correspondence. Inside the house, Libby had three "girls" working. One custom that she followed each evening was to put "on the floor, just outside her door, little notes of written instructions for each servant."[10]

There were many visitors to Lochland, all of whom were received "by the gentle spirit of hospitality and high thinking that pervaded it." One report mentioned "esoteric Buddhists, waifs and strays, and a lady from Shimla, India." But also there were "statesmen, scholars, literary lights, musicians, philanthropists, and celebrities from far and near." We will meet many such visitors in later chapters.

Libby was probably most satisfied with the women's rights reformers who viewed her home—as so many viewed her father's home in Peterboro—as a pleasant refuge for those who needed rest and rejuvenation after having been attacked on the public lecture circuit. Elizabeth Cady Stanton visited often, and spent several weeks at a time at Lochland in 1883 and 1889. Susan B. Anthony made a long visit in 1899, and both Anthony and Stanton were there together for a two-week visit in 1894. The place served as a therapeutic retreat for those needing their wounds dressed and their batteries recharged.[11]

Lochland was also a haven for Libby's extended family members. When Bessie was sick, Libby invited her to come—"we would lead luxurious lives—read lovely books + live out-doors! Dear Bessie, do come. A simple life in the open air, with freedom from all care would be so good for you." And when Gat's wife Susan D. Miller was "suffering from nervous prostration," she stayed at Lochland for months "during the winter + during the spring." In the early 1870s, Ann and Gerrit liked to visit and sleep in "the lower room" and enjoy the "Lochland Clam Bake." As they grew old,

LOCHLAND TODAY.   *AUTHOR'S PHOTO*

Libby invited her parents to live at Lochland "and give us the privilege of caring for you." They declined the offer with Gerrit citing "the press" of his business being so high that he needed to stay at his office in Peterboro. Tragically, they both died within four months of Libby's request.[12]

Lochland survived "an unfortunate fire at the Miller home" sometime in 1908. It was during this late 1890s-early 1900s time that Lochland spawned a fascinating intellectual and recreational endeavor: Fossenvue.[13]

XI

Fossenvue

Have you ever wanted to be accepted for who you really are? To feel that you are a good person with something to contribute? To feel respected and valued for your unique differences? Have you ever wished for a social setting that honors diversity and captures the essence of humanity in mutual caring?

They called it Fossenvue—an anagram of "seven of us;" a camping spot twenty miles south of Lochland on the eastern shore of Seneca Lake, where "we have each brought our faggot (bundle of sticks) to kindle the flame of friendship on the hearth of Fossenvue." It started with a group of friends at Lochland in July of 1874 who wanted to fashion a "retreat" from the normal anxiety producing and frustrating cares of life. What they built physically on Fossett's Point will be described later, because it is the quality of the relationships that developed there that is most significant.[1]

In the late 1970s, paleoanthropologist Richard Leakey revealed in Origins that the essence of humanity—the reason that the human species survived—is cooperation; the ability to share amid social complexity. For many biased, self-centered people in 21st century society, this seems like a mystic goal—beyond ordinary comprehension. This small group of radically liberal thinkers captured that human essence at Fossenvue in the last quarter of the 19th century.[2]

"Here the Great Mother [earth] takes us to her arms,
Far from the tangled world and vexing mart;

She folds us safe from fret and vain alarms
Close to the pulses of the primal heart.

Here, amid Halcyon (tranquil and happy) days and skies of blue,
We lose ourselves, we leave the world behind;
And here, Oh magic charm of Fossenvue!
A fairer world, and better selves we find."

It was a radical place that not only encouraged liberal expression, but also changed people—many of whom were women. And in the 19th century, women were not supposed to think, and speak, and act in liberal, self-ful-filling ways. The prime movers of Fossenvue were Libby and her daughter Anne. As Libby aged, Anne took over the tasks of organization and plan-ning. She believed that there was mutual benefit when diverse people inter-acted socially, especially for the achievement of empathy.[3]

The camp was used during the months of August and September, and received new guests almost every day. Fossenvue records contain a list of 534 guests between 1874 and 1900, and the camp was used until 1908. The guests were invited. Their arrival produced a "bright spot" in the day, and departure "a cloud." "The departure of the Schmidts was the only cloud which hovered over Fossenvue during this otherwise cloudless day, but that was a cloud with a 'silver lining,' the lining being the wise words + sunny presence which will long remain in our minds + hearts." Nathaniel Schmidt was professor of Semitic languages and literature at Cornell University.[4]

Louis Agassiz Fuertes visited Libby at Fossenvue several times and wrote of the "mystic power" that drew him there. As an ornithologist and artist, his work set new standards for the realistic depiction of wildlife in their nat-ural habitat. Libby's brother Greene Smith distinguished his ornithological taxidermy in the 1870s in similar realistic fashion. Perhaps Fuertes, born in Ithaca, NY in 1874, was influenced by Greene's work. He must have known of Greene; they were both lecturers at Cornell University. Fuertes' uncle was Elliot Coues, also an ornithologist, who was acquainted with Greene and wrote Field Ornithology, the book that guided Greene's taxidermy efforts.[5]

Visitors poured out their loving feelings for the place and the people in emotional poetic statements:

"O Fossenvue! in thy deep shade and brilliant sun,
Sweet sympathy I've found for all my smiles and tears,
And I shall seek thee still—O Friend of bygone years,
'Till this strange life of smiles and tears is done."

Libby expressed the connections this way:
"The warmest welcome [that] words could tell
Would be but powerless to discover
Our pleasure in the magic spell
That binds our loving hearts together."

Another visitor wrote,
"Here beneath the rustling branches
Friend to friend had side by side
Found a place in quiet converse
That the world elsewhere denied."

Anne summed up the ethos of Fossenvue quite well:
"Leave then thy ploughshare
        standing in the furrow
And come! be Nature's
        trusting child again."

They could even see humor in their new connections with wildlife. A guest named Katy wrote:
"Katy Did"
"Up among the spreading tree tops,
Under green leaves safely hid,
Sat a funny insect calling:
        'Katy didn't—Katy did.'

Though I peered into the darkness,
And the densest leaves amid,
Naught I found, tho still 'twas calling,
        'Katy didn't—Katy did.'

How knew he my name was Katie?
How knew he just what I did?
So I answered, 'No, I didn't!'
Louder piped he, 'Katy did.'"[6]

They loved to be there and were at ease to enjoy and think. They blended humanity, and nature, and humor, and serious thought in a mix that showed the tangled complexity of life, while also offering one a sense of balance. They had long fireside discussions of the political and philosophical issues of the day, and benefited from one another's perspectives. As Libby put it,

"Each day we are some good receiving...
Making this checkered life worth living."

In a poem about Fossenvue, Libby expressed well her dual purpose there pursuing intellectual endeavors and ensuring the consumption of high quality domestic "square meals." She had reminded readers in the previous stanza, "We dine, please remember, at one."

"We are fed at that hour upon Plato,
        Confucius, Kant, Locke, consommé,
John Ruskin, beefsteak, boiled potato,
        Beets, Hegel, tomatoes, Millais;
Ralph Emerson, Keats, devilled kidney,
        Spinoza, Hume, gooseberry jam,
Koot Humi, Chinese Gordon, Phil Sidney,
        Cheese, gingerbread, milk and Charles Lamb.

Oh perfect, conglomerate diet,
        Where wit is with vittles combined;
You'll never believe, till you try it,
        What vigor it gives to the mind.
Philosophers, scant though the fare be,
        Their looks of dismay may subdue;
But for me, I aver, let my share be
        Square meals and philosophy too."

FOSSETT'S POINT. LEASED IN THE SUMMER OF 1875 BY GENEVA POLITCAL EQUALITY MEMBER LYDIA PREDMORE. THE "SUMMER CAMP FOR THE ELITE" WAS ESTABLISHED AS A "LAKESIDE RETREAT" THAT CONTAINED ONE LARGE CENTRAL BUILDING, THREE TENTS AND TWO BATH HOUSES. THE "QUEEN'S CASTLE," WAS ADDED IN 1899 AS GIFT TO LIBBY ON HER SEVENTY-FIFTH BIRTHDAY.
GENEVA HISTORICAL SOCIETY

There was a pervasive sense of optimism among Fossenvue groups as they saw the good side of every person. The prevailing attitude was, "what can this person teach me?" They all enjoyed:

"The quiet sense of freedom...
That hourly stores up strength, and in my soul
The will to use the strength...
And in my heart, heart's happiest secret—peace."[7]

Although the physical characteristics of Fossenvue are less important than its social features, we must also get a view of it. In the summer of 1875, Anne Miller and her friend Ruth Ver Planck asked their fellow Geneva Political Equality Club member Lydia Predmore if she would lease Fossett's Point for use as a camp site. When a lease agreement was completed, the "summer camp for the elite" was established as a "lakeside retreat." The original camp consisted of "one large, central building, three tents and two bath houses." Another large building, the "Queen's Castle," was add-

air Solutations to the absent Friend
Where happy feet have trod this verdant floor And as the ever faithful summer sun
To each who in these five and twenty years Revives with living gold this wooded shore
Content has found within the cabin door ! Let us renew true friendships sacred fire
Which kindled here must burn for evermore.

THE CAMP. THE PURPOSE OF THE CAMP WAS ACADEMIC: TO DISCUSS LITERA-
TURE, PHILOSOPHY, RELIGION, EQUALITY, RESPECT AMONG SEXES AND ETHNICS,
AND TO REINFORCE FRIENDSHIP.   *GENEVA HISTORICAL SOCIETY*

ed in 1899 as a gift to Libby on her seventy-seventh birthday. Inside was a
"beautiful room seventeen feet square, with lofty raftered ceiling and high,
massive fireplace built of stone from [a nearby] quarry and geodes from the
lake shore...."[8]

Because Fossenvue was on the eastern lake shore, the trip from Lochland
was by boat. There was a dock on the shore of the Lochland property, and I
suspect that the Millers owned a boat, but I did not discover any record of
it. Perhaps they paid sometimes to have someone ferry them to Fossenvue.
One visitor reported that "The Sylvia with Capt. Rosca at the helm arrived
at Lochland dock." The "steamer" ran a route around the shore of the lake,
but because there was no dock at the Fossenvue stop, passengers had to be
rowed ashore. From the east side, a "zig-zag path" snaked down the hill to
the camp site from a road. A 1908 report cites two "young ladies arrived via
the Zig Zag about 10:30 to pass the day in the academic shadows of leafy
Fossenvue."

The respect folks had for the place can be felt in such comments. The
purpose of the camp was academic: to discuss literature, philosophy, reli-

QUEEN'S CASTLE

GENEVA HISTORICAL SOCIETY

gion, equality, respect among sexes and ethnics, and to reinforce friendship. One writer noted that

> "it was known for its gathering of the elite recreational, creative and artistic activity, and its association with many prominent individuals from Cornell and Hobart William Smith Colleges." The camp motto was "Kindle Friendship."[9]

The ethos of the original membership was to "be here now" and enjoy the present. Those seven members were Elizabeth Smith Miller, Anne Fitzhugh Miller, Ruth Lesley Ver Planck, Emily Dilworth Snyder, Anne Palfrey Bridge, James Fowler, and William Fitzhugh Miller. Their recreational activities at the camp included tennis, volleyball, archery, hiking, singing, sketching, piano and banjo playing, "relaxation," and, of course, swimming. "The opalescent lake proved irresistible and... the campers took a noon-day dip which they enjoyed greatly." There were also several reports of "moonlight dips." For evening relaxation, "a small bon-fire was built on the south shore, and a portion of the evening was spent sitting around it telling stories...." After the fire, "we repaired to the Cabin where [we] danced, and songs and music were greatly enjoyed."[10]

An interesting note in the 1908 Fossenvue Journal refers to Greene Smith's skiff that hung from the ceiling in his Peterboro museum called The Birdhouse. In it, he displayed over 2,000 mounted birds, some live birds, and many examples of his outdoor sportsman activities. On August 19, 1908 "while we were at tea, Predmore appeared with his team bringing the boat from Peterboro.... [We] soon put it in the water and strange to say after hanging for so many years in the 'Bird House' at Peterboro it scarcely leaked at all." Greene had died in 1880, so the boat had hung in the air for 28 years.[11]

As the summer season at Fossenvue ended, folks were disappointed. "Oct. seventh is set for the day of the camp's return to Lochland—Two weeks more of life in the open!" No more lying in a hammock between two posts in the water with just one's head out of the water. Said Anne:

GREENE SMITH'S SKIFF HUNG FROM THE CEILING IN HIS PETERBORO MUSEUM. IN-SIDE THE MUSEUM HE DISPLAYED MORE THAN 2000 MOUNTED BIRDS; THUS THE MUSEUM BECAME KNOWN AS "THE BIRDHOUSE". *GENEVA HISTORICAL SOCIETY*

"The woods are bidding us 'Good-bye'—
     Good-bye? Oh, rather say 'Good Cheer!'
For surely, 'neath the summer sky,
     We'll meet again next year."

They wrote their parting thoughts in a "Log" in the cabin in order to record "life's cheery hum." It is clear that they felt sheltered there "when we come to seek and find in nature's heart our home." They felt connected to the natural ecosystem's rhythms and to one another in a mental balance that they did not find elsewhere. One departing soul wrote,

"The effect of the sinking moon through the branches of the old Basswood + the broad band of yellow gleaming ripples which stretched across the lake seemingly just under the arch of the fallen tree—was a thing of beauty long to be cherished by all who saw it."[12]

And certainly they would all miss Libby—the Queen of Fossenvue.
"The Queen, belov'd of us all,
    With eyes dark brown in hue,
Bids welcome to both great and small
    Who love dear Fossenvue."

Guests referred to Fossenvue as if it were a loving person.
"In a peaceful and sequestered loveliness you lie...
We reach the cabin door.
Upon the threshold stands the Queen,
Benign and stately, who with smiling eye
And outstretched hands awaits us."[13]

Fossenvue still exists today. It is owned by the United States Department of Agriculture Forest Service, and managed by Green Mountain and Finger Lakes National Forests. It is open to the public.

The "Queen's Castle" was listed on the New York State Register of Historic Places on April 1, 1999, and on the National Register of Historic Places on June 1, 1999. The land on which it sits is now called Caywood Point.[14]

When renovations were being made to the Queen's Castle in 2004, Elizabeth Smith Miller's initials were found inscribed into the stone fireplace mantle, and an inscription near the roof rafters reads, "Other little children shall take my boats ashore."

This seems like Libby's message for others to carry on her optimism about the value of friendship. One guest gave her the satulation,

THIS IS THE FIREPLACE WHERE WHERE WORKERS WHO WERE RENOVATING THE QUEEN'S CASTLE IN 2004 FOUND ELIZABETH SMITH MILLER'S INITIALS INSCRIBED INTO THE STONE MANTLE. THE QUEEN'S CASTLE IS LISTED ON THE NEW YORK STATE REGISTER OF HISTORIC PLACES. THE PROPERTY ON WHICH IT SITS IS NOW CALLED CAYWOOD POINT. *GENEVA HISTORICAL SOCIETY*

"There's magic in her name
That cheers the dullest day."

In her own words, Elizabeth loved the
       "Spirit of Fossenvue,
       You come to wake
       Within my mind
       Sweet memories, and to make
       A summer in my
       soul, who for thy sake
       Have set apart
       A Sanctuary in my
       heart."[15]

THE QUEEN OF FOSSENVUE.
GENEVA HISTORICAL SOCIETY

XII

Philanthropy

It seems likely that almost any person can be philanthropic—having a desire to help others through acts of charity. In the popular mind, philanthropy is usually connected with the act of giving away money, but any resource donated for the purpose of helping others is an act of philanthropy. Elizabeth's father Gerrit Smith gave away money because that was his principal resource. Others might donate their expertise as carpenters, bookkeepers, musicians, or whatever in order to be charitable. Libby's primary resources were time and empathy, with which she was very philanthropic.

She learned the habit of philanthropy from her parents. Gerrit gave away to liberal, human rights causes about one billion dollars in today's terms, and was deeply concerned for the welfare of the "down-trodden"—anyone who was socially discriminated against and needed a boost toward equity.

Ann also donated her time to people in need. "I went today," she said, "with dear Lissie to the Devans + McDermots (Peterboro residents) and attended to their little wants as you (Gerrit) have been accustomed to do." Gerrit and Ann made regular "rounds" to people in need in Peterboro. Even their house servant Aunt Betsey did so, as she told Libby of trying to navigate through "narrow paths with high drifts... to find out... how the poor got along for some had cold houses and very little wood."[1]

Libby grew up amid this atmosphere of empathic caring for other people, and knew that her parents' ethos for life was the Golden Rule. As she stated her own guiding ethos, "He that cares only for himself has but few pleasures." As her mother noted, "My precious, weary child. How much you have gone through + are still going through to make others happy."[2]

Although the Millers' income was substantial, they considered it to be only equal to their own needs, and never donated huge quantities of money as her parents did. In order to be able to donate money, Libby engaged in fundraising projects. She used her cooking expertise to raise $1,000 from the sale of orange marmalade, invested the money until it grew to $2,500, and then offered it as scholarship funds for young women attending college.[3]

Other philanthropic efforts by Libby were quite varied. She was committed to the education of African Americans, and donated "to many schools for the colored race up to the time of her death." When the city of Geneva built a new hospital in 1893, Libby contributed $1,000 to that project. She supported the Willard Asylum for the Chronic Insane, opened in 1869 in Willard, NY, by providing "reading matter" for the residents. She provided tickets to local college students to attend presentations by suffragists at Geneva Political Equality Club events. Libby donated her time to visit prisoners at a nearby jail with other friends. On one occasion, "I went to the prison + waited half an hour, but as neither Mrs. Gibbons nor Mrs. Shepard came, I left without going 'the rounds.'"[4]

As a young woman in Philadelphia, Elizabeth was part of "a small sewing circle" that made garments for "children in a colored Sunday School." After Susan B. Anthony died in 1906, Libby gave $1,000, and her daughter Anne gave $500, to a fund in support of women's rights.[5]

When it was convenient, Elizabeth donated cash to people who were in obvious need. I found six instances of her donating money to "a poor woman" on the street, or to "a travelling musician," or "a beggar," and there were probably many more that went unrecorded. While on a canal boat for Rochester in 1841, she and Ann met "a fugitive slave woman... with her little boy two years old—we gave her ten shillings." That was an unusual occurrence, for fugitive slaves seldom used the canal for travel because of its expense and visibility.[6]

THE DRINKING FOUNTAIN THAT ELIZABETH DONATED TO THE CITY OF GENEVA.
AUTHOR'S COLLECTION

She made an interesting dontion in 1909 to the city of Geneva. On April 5, 1909, Henry H. Loomis announced his donation of land to the city as a public park. Elizabeth donated $2,500 to the city "for a drinking fountain to be placed at the entrance of the park." Originally at the intersection of Exchange and Castle Streets, it was moved in 1955 to a site adjacent to Lakeside Park. Unfortunately, it was demolished by a drunken driver in 1963.[7]

Elizabeth's most significant philanthropic legacy evolved from her connection with the wealthy Geneva nurseryman William Smith who was interested in founding a college for women. A school for men in Geneva had opened in 1796 as Geneva Academy, changing its name to Geneva College in 1822. In 1852 it was renamed Hobart College in honor of one of its early founders. By the early 1900s, Hobart College was experiencing financial difficulties. Its president, Langdon Stewardson, tried to solicit William Smith's aid, but failed. When William Smith College for Women opened in 1908—also in Geneva—the two colleges agreed to collaborate. Libby was instrumental in getting William Smith (no relation to Libby) to found the college for women.

William had visited Libby at Lochland often, and viewed her as a model of what a woman could become. He was a progressive thinker and a supporter of woman suffrage, and had hosted the 1897 National Woman Suffrage Association Convention in his Geneva Opera House. The two colleges were at first segregated, but became more integrated during the first three decades of the 20th century, finally becoming coeducational in 1941. In 1909, just two years before Elizabeth's death, the dormitory "Miller House" was erected on campus to honor her. When it opened in 1910, an oil portrait of Libby by artist Elizabeth Ross hung inside. Libby contributed money to the college to establish a continuing scholarship fund for women.[8]

Elizabeth also donated a portrait of Elizabeth Blackwell to the first dormitory at William Smith College—Blackwell House. Elizabeth Blackwell graduated in 1849 from the Medical Institute of Geneva College as the first female physician in the United States.[9]

One area toward which Libby's father Gerrit directed much of his philanthropy was the abolition of slavery. His antislavery ideas progressed into active work pursuing the goal of the eradication of slavery. Elizabeth did hold antislavery ideas, but seldom worked actively toward abolition. During her time of rearing, she was certainly influenced by the abolition work going on in what Gerrit's brother called the "Castle of Abolitionism"—the Peterboro mansion. Gerrit was an Underground Railroad "stationmaster," and successfully aided hundreds of runaway slaves traveling through Peterboro on their way to freedom in Canada. She watched as "a poor fugitive, scarred from head to foot [from whipping] found his way to our doors. A few weeks previous another had come maimed and branded."[10]

At age 12, Libby held an "abolition meeting" in her house with some of her friends, and the next year in 1836, the movement to boycott the products of slave labor pervaded the Smith home. Libby reported to her father while on a visit to relatives in Rochester that "Aunt Rebecca has been very kind to me, and has got me some other sugar." The effort of families that supported the boycott was to "use nothing that is tainted with slavery." That was sometimes difficult to carry out because it involved such staples as cane sugar, tobacco, rice, and cotton.[11]

Other factors influencing Elizabeth's antislavery attitude include her conversation with escaped slave Harriet Powell at the Peterboro mansion in October of 1839. Harriet told the two young Elizabeths—Smith and Cady—of the horrors of slavery. She also met the Fortens and Lucretia Mott while attending school in Philadelphia in 1839. Visitors at her Peterboro home included the Welds, James Caleb Jackson, Henry B. Stanton, and many other "fanatical" abolitionists who were passionately dedicated to the process of achieving "immediate abolition." She read letters from her parents when they participated in antislavery conventions. She conversed with William Lloyd Garrison, publisher of the powerful antislavery newspaper <u>The Liberator</u>, when she was in Boston, and she dealt regularly with the badgering of her cousin Elizabeth Cady Stanton to become active in the abolition movement. Stanton told Libby to read <u>Uncle Tom's Cabin</u>, and asked her to help gather signatures on petitions for the Women's National Loyal League in support of the passage of the 13th Amendment which would abolish slavery.[12]

Gerrit summed up well Libby's orientation to abolition while on a trip to Schenectady in 1843. "Our dear Elizabeth, true to her antislavery principles, accompanied me this morning to the Church of the colored people. This was not a little [task] seeing that to do it, she had to turn her back upon [her racist friends]." And given Libby's concern for proper etiquette with refined friends, this was probably difficult for her. She felt that radical action—either physical or conversational—in social circles was not preferred.[13]

One issue connected to abolition that Libby had to handle after her father's death was the writing of his biography by a friend of the Smith family, Octavius Brooks Frothingham. He was just two months younger than Libby, and had been a guest speaker in the Free Church of Peterboro. A graduate of Harvard College in 1843, and the Harvard Divinity School in 1846, Libby knew he was a trusted scholar who had been recommended to her by Gerrit's nephew John Cochrane to write Gerrit's biography. Between 1868 and 1872, Libby had heard Frothingham preach in New York City several times. For the summer of 1877, Frothingham moved from New York City to a location "near Peterboro" to write the biography. Elizabeth and Greene Smith agreed to turn over to him all of the accumulated papers of Gerrit Smith for his use in doing the research.[14]

He informed Greene that "It is at the special request of [your sister] Mrs. Miller, that I have undertaken to write a memoir of [Gerrit Smith], and I am honestly seeking the material which will enable me to do the work with entire sympathy, fullness and fairness.... Mr. Smith's... opinions, feelings and character shall be as faithfully described as the facts will warrent."[15]

And therein lay the problem. Frothingham did, in fact, write the truth about the facts of the relationship between Gerrit Smith and his abolitionist friend John Brown regarding Brown's October 16, 1859 attack on Harpers Ferry, VA. After Brown's capture, trial, and hanging, Gerrit denied that he had known anything about Brown's plan to capture the federal arsenal at Harpers Ferry. Had Smith been indicted as a conspirator, the charge would have been treason against the national government.

Actually, Smith may not have known about Brown's specific target, but he did know that Brown intended to invade the slave territory of the South in an effort to destabilize the institution of slavery. When Frothingham wrote that Smith knew more than he was willing to divulge, Elizabeth became furious and enraged. She feared for the reputation of her beloved father and demanded that Frothingham rewrite that portion of the biography.

In August of 1876, Frothingham had sent the "box of materials" back to Peterboro with the comment, "I hope the story has been written in a manner that will satisfy and please his children and friends."[16]

It had not.

Greene responded, "What a mean life of a Great and Noble Man little Frothingham has written." When Elizabeth read the section on John Brown, she was

> "surprised + pained. That such sentiments respecting Father should, virtually, be endorsed by me, is something to which I cannot consent. I wrote Mr. Putnam (the publisher) to publish no more copies until hearing from me again, + to try + recall as many [books] as possible."

Obviously, Elizabeth felt a personal investment in her father's reputation, and intended to keep the historical record purged of any hints of illegal action. She did, however, admit that "Frothingham... acted honestly—but so very unwisely!" Elizabeth and Greene knew that Frothingham had told the truth, but did not want him to, and had not told him that. There had been no contract signed between the Smiths and Frothingham of either a "pecuniary or literary" nature. As Frothingham put it,

"There was not even a casual or passing hint of an expectation that a eulogism, not a history, was wanted. That such an expectation may have been entertained appears now from the fact that certain members of the family do not think it possible that history should fail to glorify Mr. Smith."

Frothingham had offered the unpublished manuscript to all family members for their approval, but they declined that opportunity to examine it. Yet Elizabeth claimed that

"As he was not writing on his own responsibility... that chapter should have been submitted to some member of the family before going to press."[17]

What Greene and Elizabeth actually did was to produce controversy over the fact that Frothingham had written what actually happened instead of what Gerrit and his family wanted people to believe. During his lifetime, Gerrit kept a daily diary. Frothingham had that 1000+-page diary in his possession when he wrote the biography. It revealed the facts about John Brown's plans and what Gerrit knew of them. After the Smith family received the diary back from Frothingham, it disappeared. When Ralph Volney Harlow researched his biography of Gerrit Smith in the 1930s, the elderly grandson of Gerrit Smith, Gerrit Smith Miller, stated regarding the diary that he "knew nothing of it." Miller had recently turned over the collection of Gerrit Smith Papers to the library at Syracuse University, but the diary was not included. Miller's comment was an obvious lie, for he certainly knew of such a large document in his possession. We know that he did keep portions of the collection for himself that burned in the 1936 fire that consumed the Gerrit Smith mansion. The diary was probably lost in that fire.[18]

Greene wrote to Gerrit Smith Miller revealing both his attitude toward accurate history, and his attitude regarding Frothingham:

"I hope your Mother will never allow Frothy to have the book published, never mind how he may modify it. He is a dirty pup as I always thought from the day he unfortunately set foot in Peterboro."

Greene was afraid that the book would be "gratifying" to Gerrit's ene-
mies.[19]

By March of 1878, Greene and Elizabeth had decided to meet with
Frothingham and make recommendations for a revised edition of the biography. Elizabeth wrote,

> "If proper alterations can be made in the book, I shall not refuse to
> publish it.... I am willing to lay aside personal feelings in regard to...
> the disagreeable things which have been said + let the public have this
> delightful + instructive book, for such it is, but for those vile state-
> ments which shall be expunged if possible."

Greene offered the Peterboro mansion as a meeting place. They did
meet there and discuss the issue, but Greene thought him to be duplicitous.
In order to keep the first edition of the book from being sold to the public,
Elizabeth bought 350 copies and held them.[20]

As their ire over the biography grew through the month of March,
Greene vented anger and Elizabeth tried to console him. Greene wrote,

> "Frothingham ought to make a full retraction. He has shown him-
> self to be a meaner man that I set him for. He is an <u>ass</u> with education....
> The leather-lipped whelp of Hell was mousing after flaws in Father's
> character a year ago.... I have never thought Frothingham sincere in
> anything except mousing attempts to find fault in others for his own
> aggrandizement."

Greene thought the book was:

> "an insult to the memory of one of the greatest men that ever lived,
> and shows either malice or infernal weakness on the part of the writer.
> I hope that its circulation may be small. [It will] be a blight to the
> feelings of all who ever knew and loved him."[21]

Elizabeth countered,

> "This is a difficult matter to decide. So many intelligent men es-
> teem the book highly as a great addition to our literature, + presenting
> a grand noble character... that I think all personal feeling should be set

aside, + the alterations + recasting of the John Brown episode should receive our attention, + if correct + satisfactory... should be accepted."

Her fear was revealed as she acknowledged that
     "at that time... any proof of knowledge of any of John Brown's plans was sufficient to endanger a man's life."

She might also have added it was still sufficient to endanger a man's reputation.[22]

Gerrit Smith Miller was a "capital adviser" to Elizabeth throughout "the Frothingham troubles." His opinion was not favorable either. "Frothingham + Sanborn," he said, "have done what they can to tarnish Gr[and] Father's fair fame, + they would like to have us believe them his champions." As one of John Brown's "secret six" supporters, Sanborn knew the whole truth of the matter. By early April, the publisher had withdrawn all books from sale while waiting for revisions to be completed. Elizabeth noted that "Mr. F... is busy with a recasting of those obnoxious passages, + seems willing and anxious to make them what I wish them to be." By October of 1878 the revised edition had been printed, and in early November, Elizabeth approved it for distribution.[23]

One result of this fiasco over the Gerrit Smith biography was that it deprived later generations of what was probably the most valuable document in the vast Gerrit Smith Papers collection—his diary. Its chronicle of events, people and relationships within the antislavery/abolition movement would have made it one of the most valuable documents in all of American history, for he was the most powerful abolitionist in the country.

Another result was that the second edition of the biography told the story the way that the Smith family wanted it told, not the way it actually happened. Napoleon is reputed to have said that history is the fable agreed upon. In this case, Elizabeth and Greene created the past—the fable—that they wanted us to know. Before the issue with Frothingham was totally settled, the book was revised four times, and all five editions are in this author's possession. I recommend strongly that if one wants to read Frothingham's biography of Gerrit Smith, that they read the first edition *only*. It was reprinted in full by Negro Universities Press in 1969.

XIII

Dress Reform

Reformers were optimistic! They felt empowered with the belief that practical logic would lead to changes in social morals, drinking habits, dress styles, or whatever else they chose to pursue. And that made sense because they had witnessed sweeping changes in the behavior of individuals as a result of the effects of religious revivals. If preaching to individuals could change them, then why not preach to society? The flaw in that thought was that the optimistic reformers did not accurately perceive the intensity of prejudice against people who were not white and male.

In the 1840s, the antislavery movement provided impetus for feminist organizing. Women joined the movement for the abolition of slavery, but only in rolls subservient to men. Male-dominated organizations allowed women to do such "housekeeping" tasks as fund raising and gathering signatures on petitions. But this did help to break the social barrier against women participating in any activity that was political in nature. Also at this time, educational opportunities for women were expanding. Elizabeth Smith, for instance, was attending school in Philadelphia.

As women's perspectives broadened, they began to see more clearly the intensity of the bias against them held by males. As they worked to free slaves, they realized that <u>they</u> also were slaves. Elizabeth Cady Stanton stated in the first sentence of the six-volume <u>History of Wom-</u>

an Suffrage, "The prolonged slavery of woman is the darkest page in human history."[1]

One of the issues that attracted much attention as part of the early women's rights movement in the 1850s was dress reform. The current women's dress style involved a cumbersome, heavy, wide dress that inhibited physical movement, and some women were trying to change that style. There were two camps of reformers attracted to this issue: first were the "dress reformers" who believed that new dress styles would liberate women and lead to changed institutions. Second were the women's rights advocates who believed that social, political, and economic institutions would need to change before dress reform could be successfully implemented. Camp one saw dress reform leading to power; camp two saw power leading to dress reform.

Elizabeth Smith Miller actually straddled the two positions quite effectively. Although she was not a politically oriented person opting for power, she was secure enough in her own person to challenge the status quo. Women who made public statements were considered to be abnormal, shameful, and outrageous. To violate a dress code was a sign of deviance and immorality. Women, especially, were supposed to be objects to be seen, not forces to be heard. Those who did deviate from the norm were either brave or foolish because clothing represented a distinct role in the domestic vs. public sphere. The bulky dress was a symbol of intentional oppression that bound women to inferior social roles. Libby's habit of reinforcing the domestic role for women clashed with her innovative design for a short dress style that became known as "bloomers" and appeared in 1851. Her cousin Elizabeth Cady Stanton, who had known her since childhood, commented that Libby "has just made an entire new manifestation of character; one that has filled me... with wonder and surprise. I had always thought that [she] was sensitive to public sentiment; too much so, ever to strike out for herself a new path, unaided and alone."[2]

Today, it seems a shame that Libby is so well known for her "invention of bloomers," for that was a short-lived style that was only a small episode in the much larger cause of women's rights. However, it does reflect her real position in the women's rights cause. She adopted the style for practical, domestic reasons, not for political reasons, and never did become deeply involved in the battles over human rights in a democracy that followed for the remaining fifty years of her life.

Dress styles for women that prevailed in the 1840s produced a garment that, with all of its collective parts, could weigh as much as 20 pounds. It included perhaps five heavy petticoats, constraining corsets and girdles, long sleeves, and long skirts that dragged on the floor or in the mud. The outfit was "admirably suited to life as a decorative toy and little else." This style encouraged female passivity—as Elizabeth Cady Stanton wrote to Lucretia Mott, "woman can never develop in her present drapery. She is a slave to her rags." As Gerrit Smith stated the issue, women's dress style

"leaves them less than half their personal power of self-subsistence and usefulness, [and] both marks and makes their impotence."

Their clothing was

"designed to make them tiny-waisted, large-bosomed, legless creatures [with] a severe strain on the base of the spine [that] made the simplest physical exercise an ordeal." Libby wrote of a woman she saw sit down on a church pew "which groan[ed] beneath a profusion of broadcloth and silk."[3]

An important feature of the lives of oppressed people is that they find themselves shaped by forces and obstacles maintained by powerful people who are biased against them—and these barriers are intentional. The oppressed people are <u>forced</u> to expend energy battling the oppressors instead of improving themselves or their physical circumstances. Women in the early 1850s were responding to the call of the first women's rights convention held in 1848 in Seneca Falls, NY. They saw the advent of a new age of progress in which new ideas might assert power over old traditions with emancipative force. In the words of an author from that era,

"women are awakening to a consciousness of powers unused, and of fetters on mind and limb which have hitherto prevented them from doing their share of the world's work."

Now, they were ready to work.[4]

A new ethos emerging for woman shouted, "I exist, not as wife, not as mother, not as teacher, but, first of all, as woman, with a right to existence for my own sake." But an important question being asked at that time was, are women strong enough to take advantage of this opportunity? The social norms governing women specified that they were not expected to think much, or to be practical, or self-sufficient. Some women fought against the change, saying that they had all the rights they needed. Stanton called them "the mummies of civilization." And many others who hoped that the short dress would become accepted fashion would not wear it until it had become widely approved. "Thus, while nearly all admit its superiority,... few have the courage to act out their feelings and wishes."

Even Amelia Bloomer, editor of <u>The Lily</u>, admitted, "Women are not sufficiently free and independent to dare to strike for health and freedom."[5]

Although the original short dress was designed by Libby, it took on the name of "bloomers" after it appeared with an engraving and a description in the April 1851 edition of <u>The Lily</u>, a small monthly journal "devoted to the emancipation of woman from intemperance, injustice, prejudice and bigotry" published in Seneca Falls by Amelia Bloomer. When the name "bloomers" stuck, Amelia wrote,

> "At the outset, I had... no thought of setting a fashion; no thought that my action would create an excitement... and give to the style my

AMELIA BLOOMER WAS EDITOR AND PUBLISHER OF THE LILY, A SMALL MONTHLY JOURNAL "DEVOTED TO THE EMANCIPATION OF WOMAN FROM INTEMPERANCE, INJUSTICE, PREJUDICE AND BIGOTRY." ALTHOUGH THE ORIGINAL SHORT DRESS WAS DESIGNED BY LIBBY, IT TOOK ON THE NAME OF "BLOOMERS" AFTER IT APPEARED WITH AN ENGRAVING AND A DESCRIPTION IN THE APRIL 1851 EDITION OF THE LILY.

FROM THE PRIVATE COLLECTION OF JODY LUCE

name [with] the credit [due] to Mrs. Miller. This was all the work of the press. I stood amazed at the furor I had unwittingly caused."[6]

The bloomer outfit consisted of a short dress to four inches below the knee, trousers gathered at the ankle, and a short coat over a shirt and small tie. Libby considered it as an expression of practical common sense, physical comfort, and convenience. Her intent was to link beauty and practicality together, thereby enabling a woman to play the role of both the bee and the butterfly.

In Libby's own words:

"In the spring of 1851, while spending many hours at work in the garden, I became so thoroughly disgusted with the long skirt, that the dissatisfaction—the growth of years—suddenly ripened into the decision that this shackle should no longer be endured. The resolution was at once put into practice. Turkish trousers to the ankle with a skirt reaching some four inches below the knee, were substituted for the heavy, untidy and exasperating old garment."[7]

THE BLOOMER OUTFIT CONSISTED OF A SHORT DRESS TO FOUR INCHES BELOW THE KNEE, TROUSERS GATHERED AT THE ANKLE, AND A SHORT COAT OVER A SHIRT AND SMALL TIE. *FROM THE WOMEN'S RIGHTS NATIONAL HISTORIC PARK*

It is likely that Libby had seen such outfits before she designed her own. While attending school in Philadelphia in 1839-1840, she saw Quaker women in very simple dress, and when on their honeymoon in Europe, Libby and Charles "visited Swiss sanitariums where women were recuperating from the ill effects of fashionably tight corset lacing." She probably also knew that Lydia Sayer Hasbrouck, a dress reformer from Warwick, NY, had been refused admission to S.S. Seward Institute in Orange County, NY in 1849 because she wore a bloomer-like outfit that looked very similar to what Libby "invented." Also, several of the utopian communities that were popular during this reform era adopted "short dress and pants" outfits for women. They could do so without much opposition because they were outside of the public sphere of established norms. The followers of Robert Owen in the New Harmony community in Indiana did so in 1825; the Oneida Community, under the leadership of John Humphrey Noyes, did so just fifteen miles from Peterboro in 1848; the Strangites, followers of James J. Strang, of the Reorganized Church of Jesus Christ of Latter Day Saints, did so in the mid-1840s in Michigan; the Water Cure Journal endorsed the short dress outfit for use at water cure facilities in 1850.[8]

Perhaps the sad fact of this history is that Elizabeth Smith Miller did not invent anything new. She was, however, one of the first women to wear the relatively new style in public situations that exposed her to intense scrutiny and criticism; she was not part of an isolated commune or religion, and was associated with the most radical leaders of the blossoming women's rights movement. Libby's short dress, therefore, took on symbolic meaning that had not been relevant to former similar efforts at dress reform. It attracted a huge amount of attention to the message of liberation, and gave the women's rights movement a much needed public boost. In short, Libby's action was a stroke of genius.

The symbolism of bloomers was enormous. The traditional dress style was a symbol of servitude and inferiority. As Amelia Bloomer noted, "We know that in dress, as in all things else, we have been and are slaves...." The short dress signaled that the old style of long dress—a symbol of male domination and superiority—was changing. Women were changing from being concerned about how they looked, to being concerned about how they felt. Social norms were changing from emphasis on what men preferred, to emphasis on what women wanted. Women who were bold enough to wear bloomers intended to signify independence and pride.[9]

Males generally felt threatened by the new style that included pants. Men were supposed to "wear the pants" in the family, and were incensed by the fact that women were usurping that symbol of power. Their response was to attach a label not to the clothing, but to the women themselves with the dually derisive label "Bloomer Girls." This degraded not only the costume, but also the women. "Girls" is a term usually reserved for immature females. The women wearing the new style generally did not refer to it as "bloomers," but as the "Reform Costume," or the "American Dress." The 1852 National Women's Rights Convention held in Syracuse was derisively called the "Bloomer Convention."

Defiant women who challenged established norms were not even considered to be women. In the eyes of males in power they became "Amazons" or "male impersonators" and were no longer considered beautiful or useful. One bloomer advocate said, "We should indeed be a free people. Freed from the petty tyranny which now rules us with a rod of iron; we should become strong and vigorous in body and mind, and independent and courageous in thought and action." The costume, said another, "is the outbirth of a state of mind which soars above the prevalent idea of the uses of woman, therefore it shocks the taste." Bloomers became a symbol of protest against male power, and an icon for the assertion of influence beyond the domestic sphere. Most of the women who adopted bloomers had family heritages of wealth and power, or higher education, or all three.[10]

Men viewed pants on women as a form of cross-dressing—an act that blurred the boundaries between masculine and feminine. If one has an intent to discriminate against a certain category of people, then a clear boundary between "them" and "others" is necessary. That is what makes discrimination against dark-skinned people so easy. If this "pants on women" style was to succeed in being accepted, men might lose this distinguishing characteristic, and no longer be able to discriminate against women effectively, thereby losing power over them. The basic issue caught up in notions of feminism, women's rights, and bloomers is not dress reform, but POWER. What Elizabeth Smith Miller confronted by wearing bloomers was not the issue of dress reform so much as the issue of the distribution of power between the sexes. And what she learned was that the intensity of sexism manifested in discrimination against women was greater than the intensity of racism against black people.

But that perception was not obtainable by most people in the 1850s. Even many women were locked onto the notion that male power was legitimate, and felt protected under its shroud. They did not see protection as a euphemism and a pretense for power. Therefore, the prescriptions of what to do about negative reactions to bloomers were feeble and impotent. Many press reports suggested that if men had to wear long and bulky dresses, dress reform would move ahead quickly. Abba Goold Woolson, teacher, author, and advocate of dress reform in the 1850s, wrote, "Were I an emperor,... it would be my sovereign pleasure to decree that the men of my kingdom should wear women's clothes for a day...." (Perhaps if she were not enmeshed in the social power norms of the day she would have written "empress" and "queendom"). And Amelia Bloomer reported,

> "Let men be compelled to wear our dress for a while, and we should hear them advocating a change as loudly as they now condemn it."[11]

But men, then as now, have difficulty empathizing with women. Even Libby's father Gerrit Smith, for instance, could not conceive of himself as a woman. He did refer to himself sometimes as a "colored man," and could therefore empathize with them—especially the young, black, runaway slaves that showed him their wounds, told him their horror stories, and ate at his table. But even with his liberal and empathic mind, he could not _feel_ the plight of women in the power grasp of men. One journalist suggested, "Let Gerrit Smith adopt the crinoline (petticoat) and swelling skirt... and clothe his pedestals in pantaletts,..." and then his ideas might change. He did support dress reform, but that was much easier than comprehending the female mind.

The essence of the entire issue of dress reform is that men were afraid of becoming subordinate—of losing their power. The potential emancipation of women was symbolized by their wearing bloomers, and men were losing the image of them as sensual toys. Perhaps a real fear was that men and women might have to switch roles. As one liberal-minded woman humorously wrote to her husband:

> "Now then, my dear
> We'll smoke and cheer and drink our lager beer;
> We'll have our latch-keys, stay out late at night;
> And boldly we'll assert our female rights;
> While conquered men, our tyrant foes,
> Shall stay at home and wear our cast-off clothes,
> Nurse babies, scold the servants, get our dinners;
> 'Tis all that they are fit for, wretched sinners!"[12]

Most of the leaders of the dress reform movement recognized that imbedded in it was the issue of the strength of women themselves. The noted abolitionist and suffragist Lucy Stone knew that

> "Her miserable style of dress is a consequence of her present vassalage, not its cause. Woman must become ennobled in the quality of her being. When she is so,... she will be able, unquestioned, to dictate the style of her dress."

And Lydia Sayer Hasbrouck, editor of The Sibyl, a dress-reform newspaper named for a mythical Greek prophetess, wrote that "Woman's strife for public power must ever remain crippled until she shows to the world that she has the strength to sustain an individualized character." She held women responsible "for consenting to be oppressed." Libby's father also noted, "What ever the moral war, those who wage it must first conquer themselves." And his colleague in abolition Frederick Douglass, also a supporter of women's rights, said in a speech in 1857, "Who would be free, themselves must strike the blow." And some women were prepared to strike against the tyrant of fashion. Although Libby's reasons for wearing bloomers were more practical than political or philosophical, the logic for doing it was clear: discrimination hurts![13]

The traditional and "fashionable" dress style used as much as 35 yards of fabric, and could weigh 20 pounds—with a very tight corset underneath. Multiple layers of petticoats might be required to achieve the preferred "balloon" effect hanging from an 18 to 20 inch waist. The physical results were devastating to health. Tight corsets at the waist displaced visceral organs. Ribs overlapped one another; the liver was displaced below the ribs; the spleen became atrophied; the womb was pressed downward; impeded circulation of blood damaged organ function; abdominal muscular walls became inert; tight garters interrupted circulation in the legs. The result was "disorders that have won the disgraceful appellation of women's diseases."[14]

Elizabeth Cady Stanton groused that "Every vital organ is somewhat displaced by whalebone corsets." Mary J. Stafford-Blake, a Union army nurse who became professor of Women's Diseases at Boston University School of Medicine, illustrated the issue metaphorically:

"The thumb-screws of the inquisition might have been more painful to bear, but they certainly produced less harm than do the unyielding steels of her corsets, and the firm plates of metal... between which she is... cruelly pressed, and often so smugly that an impression of her fetters is indented into the flesh."[15]

Amelia Bloomer editorialized in The Lily that "distorted spines, compressed lungs, [and] enlarged livers" do not allow women full expression of their inherent capabilities. "Women cannot be free or great with limbs swathed in long skirts, the vital organs compressed to half their natural size,... and a grievous weight hanging upon them and dragging down the whole form. She cannot be healthy in body or mind,... while thus enslaved."[16]

Abba Goold Woolson, chair of the Dress Reform Committee of the New England Women's Club, pointed out that

"American ladies are known abroad for two distinguishing traits,... their ill-health and their extravagant devotion to dress [that shows] reckless disregard of hygienic rules.... Admitting... that the undoubted ill-health of our countrywomen is a national injury and a national disgrace, we should feel called upon... to do everything in our power to remove the causes which induce it [such as] our present pernicious style of dress."[17]

No wonder Libby was searching for something more comfortable!

Her work inside and outside of the house was made to be both difficult and dangerous because of the clothing that she felt forced by custom to wear. Summoning her courage in the fall of 1850, she charged forth into the social whirlpool. Feeling "dissatisfaction with myself," she said,

"for submitting to such bondage... I wanted some kind of a dress which would enable me to go up stairs with both hands full in comfort. With my long gown I could not take the baby on one arm and a lamp in the other and go up the stairs without running the risk of being tripped up, which might result in burning the baby, myself, and the house."[18]

Following the first Women's Rights Convention in Seneca Falls in 1848, the 1850s became an era of expansion for the duties and responsibilities of women beyond the domestic sphere. This would require, as Frances Willard, woman suffragist and president of the Woman's Christian Temperance Union put it, discarding the "hampering and grotesque dress of women—the worst bondage from a barbarous past that still enthralls us...." Boston M.D. Mercy B. Jackson agreed that women should "throw off all customs that tend to cramp them in any direction, and should endeavor to retain only such as liberate and enlarge their powers, and tend to invigorate both mind and body."[19]

These were certainly Libby's practical goals, and if the new style were to have a more far-reaching effect on the achievement of women's rights, so much the better. She <u>was</u> concerned about "indecent exposure" because of the possible "prurient peering" at ankles by over-active "male imaginations." But there was enthusiastic acceptance of the style within the circle of dress reformers. Amelia Bloomer rejoiced,

> "We shall no longer have our dresses drabbled in the mud, or half the depth of them wet with snow,... and we can even sit down in a puddle of tobacco juice without endangering our Sunday suit.... Small waists and whalebones can be dispensed with, and we shall be allowed breathing room; and our forms will be what nature made them."[20]

It appeared to some that one of the biggest stumbling blocks to the success of bloomers was women themselves, who would, according to Gerrit Smith, need first to become "mentally free of the bondage to men." Only then could she be "deeply conscious of her equality with man, [and] be determined to assert it in the face of ridicule...." But one must ask, how could she become "mentally free" in the face of abuse? Men who felt threatened by the obvious independence symbolized by pants on women made it expensive in many ways for the women to keep wearing them. The opposition to bloomers became intense.[21]

One opposition camp recognized that the issue of dress reform was being politicized and feared the potential redistribution of power. Gerrit Smith became concerned that the backlash from opposition to fashion change might impair the future of the woman suffrage movement. Some complained that women were trying to become men and take over societal leadership. Would emancipated women cause men to become subordinate?

Others claimed that homely women were using bloomers to attract male attention. The ultra-conservative position was well stated by Gerrit Smith's distant cousin George Fitzhugh, a proslavery apologist and author. He claimed that a collective, group-based decision of society is infallible,

> "and to differ with it is heresy or treason, because social discord inflicts individual misery, and what disturbs and disarranges society impairs the happiness and well-being of its members.... The unlimited right of private judgment [has] borne no good fruits.... Infidels, Skeptics, Millerites, Mormons, Agrarians, Spiritual Rappers, Free Negroes, and Bloomers disturb the peace of society, threaten the security of property, offend the public sense of decency, assail religion, and invoke anarchy."[22]

This conservative mind-set spawned a lot of name-calling of those women who wore bloomers. One editor said that "the outfit made a woman look like a beer keg balanced on two corks," and was pleased that "The ladies of this village—bless their little hearts!—have too much modesty and good sense to don as unbecoming a dress as this new fangled concern. While it may be suitable for unattractive women, the ladies of our own village have no need of a clownish style to attract attention."[23]

A Syracuse editor referred to women as "The Bloomers [who] were in session in our city yesterday" at a convention. "Half the human race," he said, "has just held its annual convention at Syracuse....—a petticoat parliament [attended by] these Amazons of the New World...." Men of the press were particularly cruel in their depiction of women in bloomers as "vulgar women whose inordinate love of notoriety is apt to display itself in ways that induce their exclusion from respectable society," by having "betrayed them into a masculine pugnacity." Would that notion not disqualify most men, also?[24]

When Amelia Bloomer spoke at a temperance meeting at the Brooklyn Institute in December of 1853, she also was subjected to name-calling. An editor noted that her costume

> "gave her an... eccentric and brigandish appearance, somewhat like a combination of the peculiarities of a Turkish Sultan [and] an Italian market woman."

Stanton wrote to Libby that her "dress was a subject of the severest animadversions" (criticisms), and that she had become "wearisome to be forever warding off attacks." Amelia Bloomer agreed that she also was tired from having "ventured to stand... the indecent sneer of vulgar ignorance."[25]

In addition to the "vulgar" name-calling were the editor attacks on the costume itself. Some saw it as "hideous, and offensive to the eyes." Others mentioned women who were "most indecent," or attracted "considerable curiosity." One attack that tried to substitute humor for viciousness appeared in the New York Times:

> "The other day that curious anthropoid, Miss Dr. Mary Walker, was bitten by an injudicious dog. The thoughtless person, on hearing of this incident, will, of course, feel some natural pity for the dog.... The biter of... Dr. Walker will doubtless contract her peculiar insanity.... Had Dr. Walker worn the ordinary garments of her... sex, she would not have been bitten.... The Dress Reformers will learn from this... incident that they can wear a 'garmenture of dual form' only at the cost of being bitten by hungry dogs. Prudence will therefore suggest that they make their 'garmenture' of sheet iron. Two lengths of stove-pipe would possess the duality [for covering the legs] for which they clamor."[26]

These conservative critics would point out that a woman's chief domestic responsibility was to find a man who was reputable in terms of money, land, a job, good morals, non-violence, soberness, and good manners. Wearing "different" clothing might not aid that process. Clothing makes a loud public statement, and being seen in "ridiculous" clothing would embarrass one's whole family—especially the males, who were supposed to be in control of the females. Wearing bloomers, therefore, was a move that was taboo. Even at age nine, Libby's brother Greene was already indoctrinated with social custom.

> "Now sister, take off those old pants
> And put on decent dresses
> And spirits your sweet dreams will haunt
> If you only wear long dresses."[27]

It was likely that Elizabeth Smith Miller's wearing of bloomers would attract much interest. Her social position included connections with nationally known and powerful human rights activists in both the abolition and women's rights movements, so her actions were followed closely as representing that sphere. Reactions to her, however, were not always positive. Her mother Ann said of one of their trips to New Jersey,

"Poor Lissie's dress undergoes all sorts of criticisms. Even those who approve suggest various improvements. Those who disapprove look solemn and pained." She regularly had to deal with "the jeers fools always throw at those who have independence enough to adopt a new improvement that is both convenient and useful."[28]

Cartoonists expressed a clear bias against bloomers.

BLOOMERISM - AN AMERICAN CUSTOM.

BLOOMERISM——AN AMERICAN CUSTOM.

TOP: "A QUIET SMOKE." CARTOON BY J. LEECH. BOTTOM: THE CAPTION OF THIS CARTOON READS IN ALL CAPS: ONE OF THE DELIGHTFUL RESULTS OF BLOOMERISM -- THE LADIES WILL POP THE QUESTION. ALL ILLUSTRATIONS ON THESE FACING PAGES FROM MR. PUNCH'S VICTORIAN ERA, 1851.

But Libby kept at it, hoping, in her words, to "reach a plane where fashion [would] no longer enslave her." Of the old style, she said,

"It is a sad fact that in modes of dress we have no taste [for the practical]; the most hideous costumes become beautiful in our eyes if they are only fashionable."

But all reaction was not negative. There were those who approved.[29]

Amelia Bloomer, of course, was a major supporter of dress reform. Born in 1818 in Homer, NY, she attended the 1848 women's rights convention in Seneca Falls. In 1849 she began publication of a temperance newspaper called <u>The Lily</u>. It was "Devoted to the Interests of Woman," and claimed to be "A monthly Journal devoted to the Emancipation of Woman from Intemperance, Injustice, Prejudice and Bigotry."[30]

In early 1851, Libby visited her cousin Elizabeth Cady Stanton in Seneca Falls while wearing her newly developed "short dress costume." Stanton took Libby to the local post office where Mr. Bloomer as postmaster kept open a "Ladies Exchange" where women met "to read their letters, write replies, and exchange salutations...." There, Stanton introduced Libby to Amelia Bloomer. Enthralled with Libby's new outfit, Amelia published an article about it in <u>The Lily</u>, after which her subscription number jumped from 500 to over 4,000. Because of that article, the name "bloomer" was attached to the new style which soon appeared in cities all over the northeastern United States, and in London.[31]

<u>THE LILY</u>: A MONTHLY JOURNAL PUBLISHED IN SENECA FALLS, N.Y. IT'S TAGLINE WAS: DEVOTED TO THE EMANCIPATION OF WOMEN FROM INTEMPERANCE, INJUSTICE, PREJUDICE AND BIGOTRY. AMELIA BLOOMER, EDITOR AND PUBLISHER. AUGUST 1852, VOL. 4, NO. 8.

Bloomer said of the new style, "I found the dress comfortable, light, easy and convenient, and well adapted to the needs of my busy life. I was pleased with it... and so would not let the ridicule or censure of the press move me. Such as:

> "Heigh ho! Carrion Crow,
> Mrs. Bloomer's all the go.
> Twenty tailors take the stiches,
> Mrs. Bloomer wears the Breeches."

When the Bloomer family moved to Council Bluffs, IA in 1855, the theme of The Lily was adopted by Lydia Sayer Hasbrouck in The Sybil, created in 1856 as the official publication of the Dress Reform Association which was established that year at the Glen Haven Water Cure by former Peterboro resident James Caleb Jackson. This new organization's purpose

SHORT DRESSES.

We are glad to see that several of the most respectable ladies of our village possess sufficient independence to show their disregard of the imperious mandates of Fashion, and consult comfort and convenience in the matter of dress. It is now quite common to see the short dress and pantalettes in our streets, and it is admitted by nearly all that they are a decided improvement upon the *draggling* style. Indeed, they are very generally admired, and we hope that occasional rude and insulting remarks from blackguards, and the annoying conduct of ill-mannered boys, will not discourage the ladies in their attempt to introduce a wholesome and much needed reform.
[Seneca Co. Courier.

We are pleased to learn that some of the ladies of Seneca Falls have commenced a reform in the style of female attire. We have no certain idea of the style introduced, but suppose it to be that of the short dress and Turkish trowsers—the most beautiful and graceful female dress in the world. The moral courage and firmness in thus breaking ground against the street sweeping drapery of fashion, demands our admiration. Were the new style to be adopted here, the street Commissioner would sue the wearers for damage. The cleaning of sidewalks and crossings would then be thrown upon the city.
[Cayuga Chief.

NEWSPAPER COLUMNS, BOTH TITLED SHORT DRESSES, APPEARED IN TWO CENTRAL NEW YORK PAPERS - THE SENECA COUNTY COURIER AND CAYUGA CHIEF.[33]

was to support "reform in women's dress, especially in regard to long skirts, tight waists and all other styles and modes which are incompatible with good health, refined taste, simplicity, economy and beauty."[32]

There were some small newspapers in central New York that supported the bloomer dress design. Two of them were the Seneca County Courier and the Cayuga Chief. Their short articles are found on page 139.[33]

Amelia Bloomer responded cynically to the Courier article, written by a male, that she was surprised that "our self-constituted lords and guardians" had approved of it, so now "we suppose there will be no harm in our doing so.... This only shows that women should not dare to make a change in their costume till they have the consent of men—for they claim the right to prescribe for us in the fashion of our dress as well as in things else."[34]

Elizabeth Cady Stanton was also a major supporter of bloomers—a loud one! Early on she had made the point that the corsets and long dresses inhibited a woman's comfort and movement so much that she needed a man's help all the time, thus contributing to his opportunity to dominate. And she knew what kind of fortitude it would take for the bloomer fashion to be approved. "Woman will never hold her true position, until by a firm muscle and a steady nerve, she can maintain the rights she claims.... But she cannot make the first move... until she casts away her swaddling clothes." She was afraid they might be like the fox in the fable who, having cut off his tail, had to persuade the others to do it so that he could be accepted. "As we have performed this surgical operation on our entire wardrobe, nothing remains for us to do but to induce as many as possible to follow our example. We can have no peace... until we cut off the great national petticoat. God grant that we may be more successful than the fox."[35]

As Stanton wore the bloomers through the fall of 1851, she hardened her determination to withstand the ridicule, and was pleased to see some progress in public acceptance. She thought that her persistence might cut her off from some of her friends, but piped, "if my friends cannot see me in the short dress, they cannot see me at all." She found acceptance at a dance, and on the street in Skaneateles, and by April of 1852, she was telling the public through The Lily, "Evils can never be remedied by a supine endurance of them. Shall I who see the truth never proclaim it, nor live it, because the mass are not ready to go with me?... Shall we through fear of ridicule, sail on with the multitude, doing no good work for those who come after us, whilst we are in the full enjoyment of blessings won for us by the heroes of the past?

"Does woman crave no higher destiny than to be a mere framework on which to hang rich fabrics to show them off?"[36]

A year later in May of 1853, Stanton begged Libby to

"Stand firm a little longer, dear Liz, and we shall be a respectable majority—respectable and respected. I love what I suffer for, and I have suffered a good deal for this dress."

In the end, as we shall see, Libby wore bloomers for a longer period of time than did Stanton.[37]

Another supporter of the bloomer campaign was Libby's father Gerrit. He and his cousin Elizabeth Cady Stanton had a friendly argument about his support because early on he felt that changing the dress style would change people's attitudes about women. That seems a bit simple-minded, and she let him know it. Six years into the bloomer issue he realized that

"Your dress movement involves the whole woman's rights cause. The woman whose soul is capable of casting from her person the absurd and degrading dress,... can aid that cause. No other woman can."

Gerrit attended and spoke at a dress reform convention in Canastota, NY in January of 1857. Dr. Mary Walker, a physician, suffragist, and dress reform advocate, also spoke there. And at a similar convention in Syracuse, "A letter about a yard long, was... read from Gerrit Smith. He was in favor of short dresses, short hair, and short everything."[38]

Fortunately for Libby, she lived in an approving environment in Peterboro, and when she traveled, she was able to peacefully absorb the criticism. Even her husband Charles approved of her bold move, writing as she walked through the Peterboro snow drifts in March,

"'Twas on a cold + stormy night
Long after light of day,
My Bet set out to show her might
And break the drifted way.

She stem'd along the burried fence
Nor heeded sluice or ditches.
Her courage came, I know from whence
Her breeches, aye her breeches."

But the hope that had blossomed early in the dress reform movement with

"Sound the loud timbrel o'er
Erie's broad sea,
The skirts will be shortened—
Our women be free."[39]

faded as the years passed, as even the most passionate followers gave up the bloomers.

Shortly after the bloomers first appeared in public, one newspaper editor commented,

"We do not see any reasonable chance for the adoption of the Bloomer costume which although neat, comely and convenient, is so susceptible of ridicule that the great majority of our women shrink from the ordeal which they must pass through in habituating themselves and the public to the change."

Of significance in this quote is the reference to "our women." The male editor implies possession of women with power of ownership, thereby exposing two important facts about the dress reform issue. First is the intent of males to possess females; second—and this will become clearer later—is the legitimation by women of that attitude.[40]

Among women, there were two avenues of opposition to wearing bloomers. Some opposed the practice on the aesthetic grounds that they were not attractive or beautiful. Others opposed on the political grounds that they detracted attention from the message of the implementation of human rights.

In the latter group are those who would agree with Amelia Bloomer that "the dress was drawing attention from what we thought of far greater importance—the question of woman's right to better education, to a wider field of employment, to better remuneration for her labor, and to the ballot for the protection of her rights." As Susan B. Anthony said, "The attention of my audience was fixed upon my clothes instead of my words." Following the 1854 women's rights convention in Albany, she decided to stop wearing bloomers, saying, "I found it a physical comfort, but a mental crucifixion."[41]

By mid-1853, Elizabeth Cady Stanton was still wearing bloomers, but wondering if it was worth the pain. She told Libby, "For the present we must let these narrow-minded and unfair critics rage." She had faced the bias of her father, her husband, and the public, and told Susan B. Anthony, "I never felt more keenly the degradation of my sex.... One might as well work with a ball and chain." When she did stop wearing the bloomer design in the fall of 1853, Stanton lengthened her dress, but still kept it "within one inch of my boot tops" so that it would not drag on the ground.[42]

Those women who opposed bloomers on aesthetic grounds did so usually because of its tendency to expose the upper leg when sitting down. The pantaloons were tied onto the lower leg, covering skin from the ankle to the knee. In some designs the upper leg could be exposed, as Henry B. Stanton pointed out, "To the delight of those gentlemen who are anxious to know whether their lady friends have round and plump legs, or lean and scrawny ones." Some women thought this to be "neither artistic nor attractive." Elizabeth Smith Miller was one of them. When she did stop wearing bloomers in 1858, it was "not because of the ridicule it brought down upon her, nor the howling mobs which sometimes surrounded her, but because it was 'inartistic.'" To continue wearing them made her appear to be fanatical, which she felt was not "womanly or becoming."[43] In her own words,

"The dress looked tolerably well in standing and walking, but in sitting, a more awkward, uncouth effect, could hardly be imagined—it was a perpetual violation of my love of the beautiful. So, by degrees, as my aesthetic senses gained the ascendancy, I lost sight of the great advantages of my dress—its lightness and cleanliness on the streets, its allowing me to carry my babies up and down stairs with perfect ease and safety, and its beautiful harmony with sanitary laws. Consequently the skirt was lengthened several inches and the trousers abandoned. As months passed, I proceeded in this retrograde movement, until, after a period of some seven years, I quite 'fell from grace' and found myself again in the bonds of the old swaddling clothes—a victim to my love of beauty."[44]

The decision by even the most passionate dress reform advocates to go back to the old style of longer dresses was, as they put it, to concede the loss of a battle in order to be more effective at fighting the war for women's rights. But no matter how one tries to rationalize the retreat, it must be acknowledged that men were awarded the victory. For a few years in the early 1850s, women had a heady sense of victory over the tyrant of fashion and the power of men, but they relinquished it in favor of their own subjective judgments of beauty and modesty, finding themselves still in the relentless power grasp of males. In spite of the powerful potential of a collectively based social movement, the tyranny of custom prevailed. The larger women's rights movement plodded on into the present time, but the political significance of dress reform died. "Bloomers" of some type were still used for some less significant reasons.

Some communes adopted styles of dress that were somewhat like bloomers. The Oneida Community near Sherrill, NY used "short gowns

The Oneida Community near Sherrill, NY used "short gowns or frocks, with pantaloons" starting in 1849 even though Oneida Community women objected to the women's rights movement, and after the departure of its founder John Humphrey Noyes in 1879, women there adopted the long dress. *From the collection of Jody Luce*

or frocks, with pantaloons" starting in 1849. This was a practical move to enable women who lived there to perform traditionally masculine tasks. Although some have suggested that it was an effort to achieve equity between the sexes, men certainly dominated most aspects of life at the Oneida Community. In fact, most Oneida Community women objected to the women's rights movement, and after the departure of its founder John Humphrey Noyes in 1879, women there adopted the long dress.[45]

At the Glen Haven Water Cure near Dansville, NY in 1856, James Caleb Jackson and Harriet Newell Austin adopted for their residents a modified version of bloomers that they called the "American Costume." Austin had graduated from Dr. R.T. Trall's Hydropathic College in New York City, eventually becoming a public speaker on dress reform. She and Jackson co-edited the journal Laws of Life and Journal of Health in which they advocated dress reform.[46]

Such efforts at dress reform at communes and sanatoriums were not influential beyond their borders due to their intent to remain aloof from political processes.

Some athletic activities in which women participated in the late 19th century also adopted the use of short skirts and/or pants for practical reasons. An

1868 WOMEN'S BASEBALL GAME IN PETERBORO, N.Y. *COURTESY OF THE NATIONAL BASEBALL HALL OF FAME LIBRARY, COOPERSTOWN, N.Y.*

interest in bicycling in the San Francisco area in the 1890s resulted in the popularity of a "bifurcated," pants-type garment for women, and baseball caught the interest of women in Peterboro in 1868. The captain of the Peterboro Women's Baseball Club was Libby's daughter Anne Fitzhugh Miller. Their uniform consisted of "short blue and white tunics, trimmed, white stockings and stout gaiter shoes… neat, easy, and exceedingly beautiful."

For women to play baseball was a radical thought in the 1860s. What Nannie's team symbolized was "the radical reconception of women's roles that occurred in Peterboro. [The game was] a manifestation of their rights in the public sphere…." One report of the game noted that the women players were "in full possession of the public square… while the boys were quiet spectators of the scene." And these women were noted to have "arrived at considerable proficiency in play."[47]

Although Libby did not wear bloomers regularly again after 1858, she did maintain an interest in the issue of dress reform. In August of 1892, just before her 70th birthday, she traveled to Washington, D.C. to attend "a symposium on the question of dress reform." And the legacy she left in Peterboro has inspired others. In the early 1980s, a small group of women residents of Peterboro established the "Elizabeth Smith Miller Project." Dorothy H. Willsey, Prudy Fanning, Mary Brown, and Dorothy's three daughters Nell, Gwen, and Paige had three sets of goals for their "ESM Project":

The ELIZABETH SMITH MILLER PROJECT is devoted to the preservation of people and places. There are three major goals of the ESM PROJECT:

SOCIOLOGICAL:

To support the Task Force Against Domestic Violence—Madison County

     To begin and operate a safe home program for battered persons

     To initiate a center for reflective doing

     To restore for the work ethic a respect

     To nurture interdependent living

HISTORICAL:

To preserve and present the history of the environs, work, and legacies of Ms. Miller and her family, and the influence of that history.

EDUCATIONAL:

To heighten public awareness of sociological and historical factors

To support the educational advancement of rural people of Peterboro

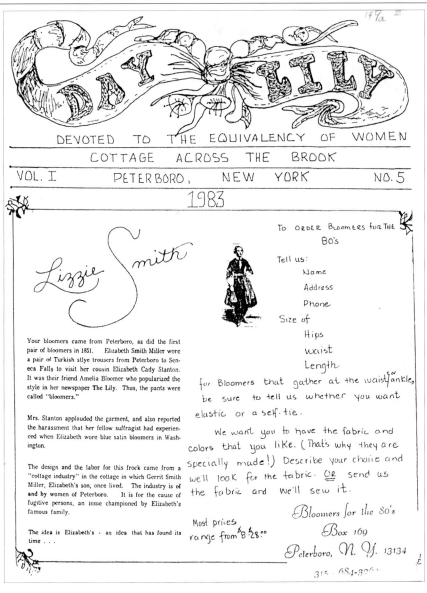

DAY LILY: DEVOTED TO THE EQUIVALENCY OF WOMEN, COTTAGE ACROSS THE BROOK, PETERBORO, N.Y.

LEFT TO RIGHT: MIRIAM O'DONNELL OF
ROCHESTER, DOROTHY H. WILLSEY-DANN
OF PETERBORO, AND JODY LUCE OF PETER-
BORO.   *FROM THE AUTHOR'S COLLECTION*

Their Project spawned a business called "Lizzie Smith Fashions," the profits of which supported "the cause of fugitive persons, an issue championed by Elizabeth's famous family." The "fugitives" in this current case were not former slaves, but battered persons. They also printed a periodical called the "Day Lily" to spread information about their business and their goals.[48]

In related activities, Prudy Fanning and Dorothy H. Willsey organized and administered "Historical Daze" at Peterboro, the proceeds of which were to benefit the Madison County Task Force Against Domestic Violence. Also, a group of 30 women aged nine to 50 marched while wearing bloomers in the Convention Days Parade in Seneca Falls in 1981, and in a few subsequent years. And in celebration of Libby's lifestyle and accomplishments, Peterboro resident Jody Luce has since 2008 managed an annual "In The Kitchen Tea"—one for children, and one for adults—that features each year the honorable achievements of a woman of historical importance, and recognizes the impact of the image of the bloomer style in bringing public attention to present social needs.

By the 1900s, opportunities for women had improved regarding property ownership, higher education, career choices in professional and management fields, and, in some locations, voting. Libby died in 1911, so she did see some of these changes. And interestingly, improvements in clothing style played almost no part in the emancipation of women. It was the social emancipation itself that brought greater changes in dress styles than the most passionate of the early dress reformers could have imagined. Libby said in her old age, "All hail to the day when we shall have a reasonable and beautiful dress that shall encourage exercises on the road and in the field—that shall leave us the free use of our limbs—that shall help and not hinder our perfect development."[49]

What Libby might feel and say about women's clothing in this 21st century we can only speculate, but she would probably not see it as "hindering" much of anything. To honor Libby's legacy in the dress reform movement, the New York State Governor's Commission Honoring the Achievements of Women placed a historical marker at the Miller family home in Peterboro on October 28, 1998. Present at the event were representatives of that Commission, the Madison County Historical Society, the Peterboro

Historical Society, the Smithfield Community Association, and the Lizzie Smith Project leaders from the 1980s.

Although the dress reform movement of the 1850s might not have had a huge impact on the styles of the day, it was important in helping to launch women into the world of politics in preparation for their next big battle: the pursuit of woman suffrage.

To honor Libby's legacy in the dress reform movement, the New York State Governor's Commission Honoring the Achievements of Women placed a historical marker at the Miller family home in Peterboro on October 28, 1998. Present at the event were representatives of that Commission, the Madison County Historical Society, the Peterboro Historical Society, the Smithfield Community Association, and the Lizzie Smith Project leaders from the 1980s.

XIV

Political Interests

Political activity did not hold much interest for Elizabeth Smith Miller. Like her father, she only became involved in it when she felt that she had to. She was always liberal-minded, but not often politically motivated. One visitor to Lochland characterized Libby as being interested in

> "intellectual culture and genuine moral elevation. Being in political faith 'democratic,' [she] was hospitable to intellect and talent,... cherished great literature, [and] valued bold and iconoclastic thinking."[1]

Libby learned this type of thinking in Peterboro, where she met and talked with all kinds of radicals and so-called "fanatics" who were actually speaking and writing about such revolutionary ideas as ending the madness of slavery, stopping the epidemic of drunkenness, allowing women to speak in public, and maybe even to vote! In the first volume of the <u>History of Woman Suffrage</u>, Elizabeth Cady Stanton wrote about the social radicalism of central New York State, noting,

> "Here the first Woman's Rights Convention was held, the first demand made for suffrage, the first society formed for this purpose, and the first legislative efforts made to secure the civil and political rights of women.... Here too the pulpit made [its] first demand for the political rights of women. Here was the first

temperance society formed by women, the first medical college opened to them, and the first woman ordained for the ministry."[2]

And to extend that thought to the issue of slavery, it was radical thinkers and actors in central New York like John Brown, Frederick Douglass, and Gerrit Smith that made southerners so angry that they shot at northerners, thereby starting a Civil War. Had it not been for central New York, there might not have been a Civil War or a woman suffrage movement at the times that they occurred.

Living in Geneva after 1869, Libby was well aware of the major issues of the day—especially pertaining to women. They involved access to education and profitable employment, expansion of roles in religion and legal systems, equitable treatment before the law, and, of course, securing their "natural right" to vote. Through their work together at Lochland, Elizabeth Smith Miller and Anne Fitzhugh Miller "insured that the... suffrage debate would take place within a generous intellectual frame." They stimulated an atmosphere of progressive and liberal reform in Geneva and beyond by their example. As historian Robert Huff noted of their work, they "raised the suffrage issue from a 'legislative joke' to a question commanding the serious attention of lawmakers and ordinary citizens."[3]

ANNE FITZHUGH MILLER (LEFT) AND HER MOTHER, ELIZABETH SMITH MILLER AT LOCHLAND, GENEVA, N.Y. ABOUT 1908.
COURTESY OF THE LIBRARY OF CONGRESS

And importantly, they were not "ordinary citizens." They were wealthy enough to never need to hold regular jobs. They could have lived a purely recreational and aristocratic life, but they did not. They chose to donate the use of some of their resources to liberal social goals based in equity. As opportunities for women expanded in the late nineteenth century, the Millers reacted by opening avenues of progress to women searching for fulfillment. One of their colleagues in such work was Ann Preston, a medical doctor from a Quaker background who addressed those attending a woman's rights convention, noting that women needed a cause. They realized that "to follow the empty round of fashion, to retail gossip and scandal, to be an ornament in the parlor or... in the kitchen, to live as an appendage to any [man] does not fill up nor satisfy the capacities of a soul...."[4]

Elizabeth Cady Stanton had pointed out to Libby "the aimless vacuity of woman's life," and their disgusting "biennial duty" of supporting voting males "in supplying soldiers and legislators for this model Republic with its gag laws and fugitive slaves." The national legislature had passed "gag rules" that forbade the discussion of petitions like those for abolishing slavery and supporting woman suffrage. Stanton at times sought Libby's help in soliciting signatures on suffrage petitions in the local areas near Peterboro like Hamilton and Cazenovia. Libby's commitment to such active processes was not as strong as Stanton's, and just what she accomplished there is not known. Even Ann Smith felt somewhat insignificant. While nursing a sprained ankle, she chimed in regarding her husband who was to speak in Boston, "I have looked in vain to see the announcement of my poor bruised foot in the papers—alas the difference."[5]

Libby did support women's rights issues throughout her life, just not with the same degree of passion as did Stanton. Whereas Libby held low confidence in her "conversational powers," Stanton was a master of the use of words, and a powerful and convincing public speaker. Libby would stay reclusive and quiet while Stanton charged forth into teeth of public opposition and criticism.

As a center of activity on human rights issues, Peterboro offered the young Elizabeth Smith ample opportunity to learn about their significance in liberal social philosophy. Gerrit was pursuing the abolition of slavery and temperance when Elizabeth was teething. She heard human rights ideas at the dinner table and talked with the advocates in the parlor. At age 12 she was holding "abolition meetings" with her friends, and spending summer months with Elizabeth Cady.

A local antislavery society was organized in the township of Smithfield, in which Peterboro is located, in 1834, and the New York State Anti-Slavery Society held its inaugural meeting in Peterboro in 1835. Starting in 1843, "sermons" at the Free Church of Peterboro that the Smith family organized and attended were actually political pleas for human rights. Guest speakers there included Frederick Douglass, John Brown, Elizabeth Cady Stanton, and countless other agitators for human rights. Also in 1843, a Female Anti-Slavery Society was organized in Hamilton—just 14 miles from Peterboro. It is not known if Libby participated in any of these early human rights organizations, but she certainly knew of their existence and their significance.

When the first women's rights convention was held in Seneca Falls in 1848, Libby may not have attended. She <u>was</u> in communication with her cousin "Lib" Stanton about it, and, according to one report, helped Stanton organize it. She was one of the signers of "the call" for the second women's rights convention in Worcester, MA on October 23-24, 1850. Also among the signers of that call were her husband Charles Dudley Miller, and her parents Ann and Gerrit Smith.[6]

In 1868, Libby wrote a letter on behalf of women to the National Republican Convention meeting in Chicago in June, asking the party to "recognize in its platform their right to suffrage." Her letter received no recognition. As the women's rights movement heated up after the Civil War, Gerrit was speaking in support of the general idea, but would not support woman suffrage at that time because he felt that it would interfere with the achievement of black male suffrage. Libby, however, pressed on with her support for woman suffrage. When Susan B. Anthony split from the Equal Rights Association in 1869 and created the National Women's Suffrage Association, Elizabeth Smith Miller was selected as treasurer. Also in 1869, she asked her father to offer his powerful support to women's rights organizations, and to Stanton's publication <u>The Revolution</u>.[7]

In 1878 she was the Ontario County delegate to Rochester's 30th anniversary celebration of the 1848 Seneca Falls Convention, and throughout

the last decades of the 19th century she was a constant worker for and supporter of suffrage with her daughter Anne at Lochland. In 1894, she was
invited to speak at a women's rights meeting in Auburn regarding political
equality for women taxpayers. She responded (curiously) that although she
was not a taxpayer (but her family/husband was), she would speak anyway
because "my interest in the whole suffrage question is so great that I could
not decline to take part in the work organized by the women of Ontario
County." As she aged, she agreed to be an officer—perhaps of the honorary type—of the Woman Suffrage Association of America, the National
Woman Suffrage Association, and the New York State Woman Suffrage
Association. Then at age eighty-one, Libby and Susan B. Anthony were
invited to speak to the Phyllis Wheatley Club, a black women's club in New
Orleans. Evidently Susan went, and Libby did not, but the comment made
by Sylvanie Williams of the Wheatley Club is revealing regarding Libby's
reputation.

> "When women like you... come to see us and speak to us it helps
> us to believe in the Fatherhood of God and the Brotherhood of Man,
> and, at least for the time being, in the sympathy of woman."

The Phyllis Wheatley Club had been accused by the local New Orleans
Times-Democrat of racism.[8]

Given that Libby was a consistent supporter of women's rights—especially the suffrage issue—it is fair to question the degree of enthusiasm
of her support although we must keep in mind her habit of intentionally
staying in the background and out of public view.

At age 14, while visiting relatives in Schenectady, Libby wrote to her father,
> "My cousins here think with me that ladies have enough to attend
> to without 'holding forth' to larger assemblies than those collected in
> their own parlors, and by their own firesides."

What they were "attending to," of course, were domestic tasks. One
year later, Gerrit chastised the young Elizabeth for her lack of interest in
women's rights issues.[9]

There is some question as to whether Libby attended the 1848 wom-
en's rights convention in Seneca Falls. She certainly knew of it, and had

some input with "cousin Lib" in organizing it. Neither Gerrit nor Ann attended, and if Libby did, she did not sign the Declaration of Sentiments as did most of the attendees. Stanton tried to keep Libby informed about the proceedings of the women's rights movement. She wrote of the 1877 National Woman Suffrage Association convention in Washington, D.C. that she and Susan B. Anthony had spent two days and evenings talking to "senators, congressmen, judges, lawyers' wives and daughters.... Susan is completely used up." Libby did not attend.[10]

When testimony before legislative committees was necessary, it was Anne that responded, not Libby. Anne said of her mother, "In the early years of the suffrage movement, its advocates were often called 'shrieking sisters!' For more than 80 years my mother has, like 'Brer Fox,' kept on 'saying nothin'. Consequently she has not earned a place on the platform in the ranks of that denomination. Nevertheless, she is an ardent woman suffragist...." It appears that Libby's lifelong focus on domestic excellence and her probably inborn shyness regarding self-expression combined to keep her on the fringes of active and passionately emotional involvement in the bulk of the women's rights movement. She stayed just outside of the cadre of "movers and shakers" of the movement—people like Susan B. Anthony, Elizabeth Cady Stanton, and Matilda Joslyn Gage—all of whom were close by in central New York.

Always known as a supporter of women's rights—especially through her work at dress reform—Libby maintained a low social profile, and is, therefore, not usually considered to be one of the giants of the movement. Even so, she always garnered a high degree of respect from that cadre of leaders—especially Stanton who admired Libby's work on the domestic scene. When Stanton was asked to voice what she believed to be the most impressive example of heroism, she responded that "the greatest heroes are the satellites of the dinner pot and the cradle—they who toil without reward, who are sacrificed in every household, who suffer that men may shine; heroes whom none envy, to whom none build monuments, whose names even are often not inscribed on the stones which mark their last resting place." They are, she would point out, referred to as "Mrs." somebody.[11]

Although Libby shined in the domestic area and not in the political area, she did pursue women's rights from other angles, one of which was the education of women. Already covered in a previous chapter was her philanthropic support of schools for women, especially William Smith College. Her "marmalade money" supported scholarships for women, and she helped fund activities on that campus designed to broaden the perspectives of women. At her annual "piazza party" (of which we shall learn more later), she invited speakers who advocated better education for women. In 1901, Mrs. W.A. Montgomery, Commissioner of Rochester Schools, addressed Geneva Political Equality Club women on "Public schools—their influence and power in making good, intelligent citizens."

And in 1908, Hobart College president Langdon C. Stewardson's address noted that "Women have the same intellectual... powers as men, and naturally these powers and capabilities claim for themselves a theater of action.... The suppression of these faculties or... the confinement of them within certain prescribed and conventional areas means dissatisfaction, pain, distress, [and] ineffectiveness...." Stanton was pleased with Libby's advocacy of education for women and gave her high praise for supporting it.[12]

Geneva Political Equality Club Piazza Party
At Lochland, Monday, June 1st, 1908
From 4 to 7 o'clock

Baritone Songs,   .   .   Mr. Charles Meehan

Cornell Woodford Prize Address, . "Men, Women and Human Beings"
Miss Elizabeth Ellsworth Cook

Tenor Songs   .   .   Mr. George Pelzer

Address,   .   .   "The Man in the Case"
Prof. Ernest Schoder, Cornell University

Light refreshments will be served on the piazza and it is expected that the wistaria will be in bloom.

Conveyances from Seneca Street every half hour.

Tickets 25 Cents, at Miss Scott's and Lochland Entrance

MRS. W.A. MONTGOMERY, COMMISSIONER OF ROCHESTER SCHOOLS, ADDRESSED GENEVA POLITICAL EQUALITY CLUB WOMEN ON "PUBLIC SCHOOLS—THEIR INFLUENCE AND POWER IN MAKING GOOD, INTELLIGENT CITIZENS.
GENEVA HISTORICAL SOCIETY

Another of Libby's educational efforts was the Elizabeth Smith Miller Study Club. Organized in 1906 for young people over the age of sixteen, it met twice each month to study the lives of successful people. The schedule for the first and third Mondays of 1908 included Alfred Tennyson, Jane Addams, Darwin, Felix Mendelssohn, Abraham Lincoln, Susan B. Anthony, Oliver Wendell Holmes, and John Greenleaf Whittier. Its fifty students were mostly women. They also read literary works such as Harriet Beecher Stowe's Uncle Tom's Cabin, and Victor Hugo's Les Miserables. This study group also spawned a Political Equality Study Class.[13]

A fascinating legal case in which Libby became involved that had implications for all aspects of women's rights is what is known historically as "The Case of Hester Vaughn." Hester was an uneducated woman who was raped by her employer in Philadelphia. When she was found in an apartment with her dead baby, she was accused of infanticide and sentenced to death. Leaders of the women's rights movement Elizabeth Cady Stanton, Susan B. Anthony, and Elizabeth Smith Miller saw the case as symbolic of the oppression of women in a male-dominated world, and decided to use the case to highlight women's rights issues in the political, economic, and legal spheres. The Working Woman's Association, a new group spawned in the offices of Stanton and Anthony's radical women's rights journal The Revolution, took on the case as an example of injustice toward women.

The WWA called a protest meeting at Cooper Institute in New York City that was attended by over 1,000 people. Their resolution called for a pardon for Hester Vaughn based on the discriminatory practices of legal institutions that had sentenced the mother to death while allowing the father to remain untried and free. Such institutional protection of men was not only unfair, said these women, but also unjust and illegal.

The resolution for pardon was carried to Pennsylvania Governor John Geary personally by Elizabeth Cady Stanton. Governor Geary initially objected to the request, but eventually did pardon Hester Vaughn with the condition that she leave the United States. The significance of the case rests in the need for educated and empowered women who are respected by institutional leaders, and capable of asserting and defending themselves against widespread anti-woman bias.[14]

The major area where discrimination against women was most pernicious dealt with their eligibility to vote. Whereas Libby's intense concern was, of course, to acquire the vote, there was an important and long-lived anti-suffrage campaign. The two important points highlighted by the suffrage issue are the right of every adult citizen of a democracy to vote, and the ability of those in power to prevent it.

Libby spent most of her adult life pursuing suffrage for women. Men had opposed extending the right of voting to women consistently during her life. She even watched her ultra-liberal father oppose it during the push for black male suffrage just after the Civil War. She must have reacted with chagrin when the New York State Association Opposed to the Extension of Suffrage to Women was founded in 1895, and again when Theodore Roosevelt—who was President of the United States from 1901 to 1909—said of woman suffrage, "I am not an enthusiastic advocate of it because I do not regard it as a very important matter." He only highlighted the difficulty that many men had in identifying with women.

As a part of their Geneva Political Equality Club activity, Libby and Anne invited Hobart College Chaplain Rev. Joseph Alexander Leighton, professor of psychology and philosophy, to address their group in February of 1909. They knew that he was an anti-woman suffrage person, so their invitation accents their intent to hear all sides of an issue. In his presentation entitled "The Inexpediency of Woman Suffrage," he claimed that "there are no natural and inherent political rights absolutely belonging to man or woman.... Political rights... are the result of a long, slow process of social evolution." This position was contradictory to the philosophy of the Reform Era which held that every human being, by the fact of birth, is endowed by God with inalienable rights. They do not "evolve," and the only legitimate function of government is to protect these rights from abuse by biased people. Rights cannot be granted, only protected.

Leighton emphasized that

> "Universal manhood suffrage was established in this country under the influence of the mistaken theory of natural rights, and led to giving suffrage to the emancipated negroes. Both steps were mistakes.... I deem it inexpedient to admit all women to the suffrage because we are suffering now in this country from the indiscriminate exercise of the

suffrage by all kinds of men, including... voters who can be bought....
I do not believe that to multiply the number of our voters by two...
will help deliver us from any of the evils from which we are suffering.
I suppose there are... as many women who could be bought, as many
ignorant, [and] many more who are indifferent...."

Leighton's address stimulated the establishment of an anti-suffrage
organization in Geneva with an entirely female membership.

In 1893, Hobart College President Eliphalet Nott Potter visited Libby
and Elizabeth Cady Stanton at Lochland to discuss his anti-woman
suffrage position with them. I suspect he got an ear full—especially from
Stanton. The important point to note here is the institutional leadership
positions of the anti-woman suffrage men. They certainly had a high degree
of influence.[15]

As an example of the ideas promulgated by such leaders, the reaction of
Rev. Dr. S.H. Cox, pastor of the First Presbyterian Church in Brooklyn, to
a women's rights convention held in Pittsfield, MA in 1853 is instructive.
He stated that

"Women ought eminently to know their mission and their des-
tination, as ordained by their Creator; to understand correctly the
whole circle of their... duties, and... to perform them; to comprehend
aright their own appropriate spheres, and moving in them, to adorn
and enrich them with incomparable attractions; and knowing well
their... places.... And this alone is potential to keep them from those
ridiculous extravaganzas and elaborate inutilities... of the Amazonian
experimenters of our age, the silly 'bloomers,' the wranglers for wom-
en's rights, as if women had no duties...."

He obviously expected women to work hard, look pretty, and be quiet,
a common opinion for men of that time.[16]

As another example, Libby's nearby Auburn neighbor and noted prison
administrator Thomas Matt Osborne wrote to Anne in 1907,

"I do not take any real interest in the Woman Suffrage proposition
as such—it does not appeal to me.... I am wasting my time when I
devote any of it to [woman suffrage]."

Some May, Some May Not

IN THIS COUNTRY SOME *MAY*
VOTE AND SOME *MAY NOT.* THOSE
WHO *MAY* ARE:

White Men	Blind Men
Black Men	Lame Men
Red Men	Sick Men
Drunken Men	Rag Men
Deaf Men	Bad Men
Dumb Men	Dead Men

THOSE WHO *MAY NOT* ARE:

Minors	Lunatics
Idiots	Convicts

WOMEN

VOTES FOR WOMEN!

THE WOMAN'S REASON.

BECAUSE

BECAUSE women must obey the laws just as men do,
They should vote equally with men.

BECAUSE women pay taxes just as men do, thus supporting the government,
They should vote equally with men.

BECAUSE women suffer from bad government just as men do,
They should vote equally with men.

BECAUSE mothers want to make their children's surroundings better,
They should vote equally with men.

BECAUSE over 5,000,000 women in the United States are wage workers and their health and that of our future citizens are often endangered by evil working conditions that can only be remedied by legislation,
They should vote equally with men.

BECAUSE women of leisure who attempt to serve the public welfare should be able to support their advice by their votes,
They should vote equally with men.

BECAUSE busy housemothers and professional women cannot give such public service, and can only serve the state by the same means used by the busy man—namely, by casting a ballot,
They should vote equally with men.

BECAUSE women need to be trained to a higher sense of social and civic responsibility, and such sense develops by use,
They should vote equally with men.

BECAUSE women are consumers, and consumers need fuller representation in politics.
They should vote equally with men.

BECAUSE women are citizens of a government of the people, by the people and for the people, **and women are people.**
They should vote equally with men.

EQUAL SUFFRAGE FOR MEN AND WOMEN.

WOMEN Need It.
MEN Need It.   **WHY?**
The STATE Needs It.

Women Ought To GIVE Their Help.
BECAUSE   Men Ought To HAVE Their Help.
The State Ought To USE Their Help.

National American Woman Suffrage Association

REASONS FOR PURSUING THE RIGHT FOR WOMEN TO VOTE.
GENEVA HISTORICAL SOCIETY

And this was 54 years after the statement made by Rev. Cox![17]

In the 1890s, only 2.7% of women 21 or older belonged to pro-suffrage organizations. Anti-suffragists used this figure to claim that 97% of women opposed woman suffrage. Many upper class women did prefer to avoid politics, but that did not mean that they were against suffrage.[18]

The first public demand for woman suffrage appeared in Resolution #9 of the Declaration of Sentiments adopted at the first Women's Rights Convention held at Seneca Falls in 1848. It read:

"Resolved, that it is the duty of the women of this country to secure to themselves their sacred right to the elective franchise."

As the country moved toward civil war, the leaders of the women's rights movement agreed to pause their demands in favor of temporary support for the abolition of slavery. After the war, they formed the American Equal Rights Association in 1866 "to unite abolitionists and women's rights activists in one organization designed to pursue the common goal of universal suffrage." When the abolitionists refused to support woman suffrage, the women dropped out to form the National Woman Suffrage Association in 1869 to focus on an amendment to the federal Constitution. Also in 1869, the American Woman Suffrage Association was formed to focus on action at the state level. A last step in organizational activity occurred in 1890 with the merger of the last two mentioned associations into the National American Woman Suffrage Association as a unified base for political power.[19]

Success at achieving woman suffrage in the nineteenth century moved at a glacial pace. Whereas a few states or territories did achieve it—Wyoming in 1869, Utah in 1870, Colorado in 1893, and Idaho in 1896—there was virtually no movement at the national level. But as the status of women improved due to the increasing availability of education, the suffrage movement heated up in the late 1890s.[20]

Libby and Anne responded by accepting new challenges. In August of 1897, Harriet May Mills, Chairperson of the Organization Committee of the New York State Woman Suffrage Association, visited Libby and Anne at Fossenvue to encourage them to host the upcoming November convention in Geneva. They agreed to do so, and on November 3-6, meetings were held at various venues in the city (see program on next two pages), while speakers

The

Twenty-ninth Annual Convention

of the

New York State

Woman —

Suffrage

Association,

Geneva, November 3, 4, 5 and 6, 1897.

Headquarters:—The Nester Hotel.

Collins Hall—November 3, 7.45 p. m.
Smith Opera House—November 4 and 5, 9.30 a. m., and 2.30 and 7.45 p. m.

Executive board meetings at The Nester.
All other meetings open to the public.
Entrance fee of ten cents on Thursday and Friday evenings.

"Taxation without representation is tyranny."

Officers of the

New York State Woman Suffrage Association.

President—MARIANA W. CHAPMAN,
160 Hicks St., BROOKLYN.

Vice Pres't at Large—ELIZABETH BURRILL CURTIS,
West New Brighton, STATEN ISLAND.

Recording Secretary—MARY THAYER SANFORD,
20 James St., ROCHESTER.

Corresponding Secretary—ISABEL HOWLAND, SHERWOOD.
Treasurer—KATE S. THOMPSON, 50 Allen St., JAMESTOWN.

Auditors: { JEAN BROOKS GREENLEAF, Rochester.
           { ELIZA WRIGHT OSBORNE, Auburn.

Chairman of Organization Committee — HARRIET MAY MILLS, 926 W. Genesee St., Syracuse.
Chairman of Legislative Committee—MARY HILLARD LOINES, 26 Garden Place, Brooklyn.
Chairman of Press Committee—ELNORA M. BABCOCK, Dunkirk.
Chairman of Industrial Committee—HARRIET A. KEYSER, 252 W. 99th St., New York.
Chairman of Finance Committee—HENRIETTA M. BANKER, Amsable Forks.
Chairman of Committee on Work Among Children—J. MARY PEARSON, Auburn.
Chairman of Railroad Committee—JULIE R. JENNEY, Everson Bldg., SYRACUSE.

LIBBY AND ANNE FOUNDED THE GENEVA POLITICAL EQUALITY CLUB. ON NOVEMBER 30, 1897, 50 CHARTER MEMBERS MET AT THE YMCA[!] IN GENEVA AND ESTABLISHED THIS ORGANIZATION TO PURSUE EQUITY AND JUSTICE FOR ALL PERSONS WITH EMPHASIS ON COOPERATION AMONG THE SEXES. DUES WERE FIFTY CENTS PER YEAR.

WEDNESDAY, NOVEMBER 3.

AFTERNOON, 3.00-5.00.

Executive Board Meeting at The Nester.

EVENING, 7.45-9.45.

MUSIC. . . . . MANDOLIN CLUB
PRAYER, . . PRESIDENT JONES, Hobart College, Geneva
ADDRESS OF WELCOME, . MR. M. F. BLAINE, Geneva
RESPONSE, {MRS. MARIANA W. CHAPMAN, Brooklyn, President New York State Woman Suffrage Association.
ADDRESS, {MRS. LILLIE DEVEREAUX BLAKE, New York, President New York City League.
ADDRESS, {MISS ALICE STONE BLACKWELL, Boston, Editor of the Woman's Journal.
ADDRESS, {MISS SUSAN B. ANTHONY, Rochester. President National American Woman Suffrage Association.

THURSDAY, NOVEMBER 4.

MORNING, 9.30-12.00.

MINUTES. . . . MRS. MARY THAYER SANFORD
ANNOUNCEMENT OF COMMITTEES: Credentials, Resolutions, Finance, Courtesies.
ROLL CALL OF COUNTIES.
REPORT OF EXECUTIVE COMMITTEE, MRS. MARIANA W. CHAPMAN
REPORT OF CORRESPONDING SECRETARY, MISS ISABEL HOWLAND
REPORT OF TREASURER, . MRS. KATE S. THOMPSON
REPORT OF FINANCE COMMITTEE,
MRS. HENRIETTA M. BANKER, Chairman
INTRODUCTION OF FRATERNAL DELEGATES.
COUNTY REPORTS.

AFTERNOON, 2.00-3.00.

MINUTES.
REPORT OF CREDENTIALS COMMITTEE.
ELECTION OF OFFICERS.

AFTERNOON, 3.00-4.30.

MUSIC—Piano Solo, . . MISS FOWLE, Geneva
PRAYER, . . REV. MR. BALLOU, Geneva
ADDRESS, {MISS HARRIET MAY MILLS, Syracuse, Chairman of Organization Committee.
ADDRESS, . MR. CHARLES HEMIUP, Geneva
ADDRESS, . MRS. MARY LEWIS GANNETT, Rochester
ADDRESS, . REV. DR. REMICK, Geneva
QUESTION BOX.

EVENING, 7.45-9.45.

(Ten cents admission.)

MUSIC. . . DEADWOOD QUARTETTE, Geneva
PRAYER, . REV. LANSING BAILEY, Geneva
ADDRESS, . MRS. MARY SEYMOUR HOWELL, Albany
ADDRESS, . MISS JULIA R. JENNEY, Syracuse
ADDRESS, {MISS HARRIETTE A. KEYSER, New York, Chairman Industrial Committee.
ADDRESS, . MR. W. SMITH O'BRIEN, Geneva
ADDRESS, . REV. ANNIS FORD EASTMAN, Elmira

FRIDAY, NOVEMBER 5.

MORNING, 9.30-12.00.

MINUTES.
REPORT OF COMMITTEE ON WORK AMONG CHILDREN,
MRS. J. MARY PEARSON, Chairman
REPORT OF LEGISLATIVE COMMITTEE,
MRS. MARY HILLARD LOINES, Chairman
REPORT OF INDUSTRIAL COMMITTEE,
MISS HARRIETTE A. KEYSER, Chairman
REPORT OF ORGANIZATION COMMITTEE,
MISS HARRIET MAY MILLS, Chairman
PLAN OF WORK.
PLACE OF HOLDING NEXT CONVENTION.
CONSTITUTIONAL AMENDMENTS.

AFTERNOON, 2.00-4.30.

COUNTY REPORTS.
REPORT OF RESOLUTIONS COMMITTEE.
REPORT OF PRESS COMMITTEE, ELSORA M. BABCOCK, Chairman

EVENING, 7.45-9.45.

MUSIC—Chorus . . . UNION SCHOOL CHILDREN
PRAYER, . REV. A. H. BROADWAY, D.D., Geneva
ADDRESS, . MRS. MARY E. CRAIGIE, Brooklyn
ADDRESS, . MRS. IDA A. HARPER, Indianapolis, Ind.
ADDRESS, . DR. WILLIAM H. JORDAN, Experiment Station, Geneva
ADDRESS, {REV. ANNA HOWARD SHAW, Philadelphia, Vice-President at Large, National American W. S. A.

SATURDAY, NOVEMBER 6.

MORNING, 9.00.

EXECUTIVE BOARD MEETING AT THE NESTER.

and delegates "were entertained at the handsome home of Mrs. Elizabeth Smith Miller." Guests noted that

> "Lochland is so beautifully situated, surrounded by green lawns, and flowering shrubs, with a vista of the clear waters of Seneca [Lake] through the forest trees that the scene is entrancing...."[21]

PICTURE FROM ABOUT 1907 OF (LEFT TO RIGHT) ANNE FITZHUGH MILLER, ELIZABETH SMITH MILLER, MARY ANTHONY, AND SUSAN B. ANTHONY.
GENEVA HISTORICAL SOCIETY

The optimistic tone of the convention was set by the reading of an opening prayer sent from the office of Hobart College President Rev. Robert Ellis Jones: "Beat down bigotry and prejudice. Make even handed the justice to prevail between man and woman." Two days of meetings and committee reports followed by evening speakers on suffrage issues created an encouraging sense of rising enthusiasm and new possibilities in the minds of attendees. One month later, under Anne Fitzhugh Miller's leadership, Libby and Anne founded the Geneva Political Equality Club. On November 30, 1897, 50 charter members met at the YMCA[!] in Geneva and established this organization to pursue equity and justice for all persons with emphasis on cooperation among the sexes. Dues were fifty cents per year.

The original group consisted of an equal number of men and women "of public spirit and progressive principles." The leadership positions of Anne and Libby were unusual for that era. Most public work regarding socio-political affairs was the province of men, with women playing quietly supportive, dutiful roles. Anne became very active in suffrage circles after 1897. The first president of GPEC was Mrs. H.K. Clapp, the wife of a Hobart College professor, but in 1898, Anne was elected president, and remained so until her death in 1912. During that time, she was also a member of the legislative committee of the New York State Woman Suf-

Members.

Adams, Mrs. Lloyd P.
Anderson, Mr. J. B.
Allen, Mrs. O. D.
Allen, Mrs. W. H. (Syracuse)
Allen, Miss Edith D.
Allen, Miss Ethel H.
Alsop, Miss Elizabeth
Allen, Mrs. M. L.
Allen, Miss M. L.
Archer, Sarah Frances
Armstrong, Mrs. Sarah
Arnold, Miss Eliza
Baldridge, Mr. and Mrs. C. A.
Baldridge, Miss Anna
Bacon, Mrs. W. A.
Baner, Rev. G. C.
Babbett, Mrs.
Barber, Miss Clara
Blaine, Mr. and Mrs. M. F.
Butts, Mr. and Mrs. J. E. P.
Beard, Mrs. Charles
Brown, Miss Louisa
Butler, Mrs. Cornelia
Burbank, Miss E. H
Bonnett, Mr. and Mrs. W. L.
Burrall, Mr. and Mrs. C. S.
Buchholtz, Mrs. A.
Carson, Miss Isabelle
Catterson, Miss Susie
Chew, Mr. T. H.
Clapp, Mrs. M. A.
Chase, Mr. and Mrs. R. G.
Chitry, Mr. W. F.
Collins, Mr. and Mrs. L. D.
Covert, Dr. N. B. and Mrs.
Churchill, Mr. George W.
Congdon, Mr. and Mrs. C. H
Cook, Mr. and Mrs. E. J.
Collie, Dr. E. G.
Darrow, Mrs. Charles H.
Depew, Miss Frances
Fairchild, Mrs. H. E.
Fairchild, Mr. O. J.
Faulkner, Miss Frances L.
Fowle, Mrs. A. I.
Frisbee, Mr. and Mrs. A. J.
Ferguson, Miss Mary
Farwell, Mrs. John G.

Folger, Mrs. Charles
Fish, Mrs. Frank
Fairfax, Mr. and Mrs. Charles W.
Fairfax, Mr. and Mrs. George S.
Feaut, Mrs. W. H.
Foote, Mrs. J. W.
Finch, Mrs. Sarah S.
Green, Dr. and Mrs. F. A.
Green, Miss Edna
Gilbert, Miss Emma
Gracey, Mr. and Mrs. W. A.
Guile, Mr. Charles
Guilford, Mrs. Frank
Griffith, Mrs. E. A.
Graves, Mr. and Mrs. H. B.
Goodale, Miss Clara
Guether, Mrs. W. M.
Hallenbeck, Mr. and Mrs. D. W.
Haley, Mr. and Mrs. J. M.
Hardison, Mr. and Mrs. F. K.
Herendeen, Mrs. E. W.
Herendeen, Mr. and Mrs. Wm.
Herendeen, Mr. and Mrs. F. A.
Henderson, Mrs. S. E.
Harman, Mr. and Mrs. M. H.
Haskins, Mr. and Mrs. George
Haskins, Mr. Charles
Hemiup, Mrs. Maria R.
Hemiup, Mr. Charles
Hemiup, Miss Eva
Holman, Miss J. E.
Howe, Miss Nettie
Henry, Mrs. Lynn
Henry, Mr. and Mrs. D. H.
Henson, Mrs. Robert
Henion, Mrs. Cornelius
Hopkins, Miss L. G.
Huntington, Herbert (Canandaigua)
Humphrey, Mr. and Miss. W. F.
Howland, Mrs. C. W.
Hubbard, Mrs. T. S.
Hubbard, Miss Florence
Hoke, Mrs. Charles H.
Hart, Dr. and Mrs.
Herrick, Miss L. W.
Jacobsen, Heinrich (Rochester)
Jennings, Dr. Mary
Jones, Mrs. Rosaline E.

(8)

Jones, Mrs. W. C.
Kellner, Mrs. Rose
Keyes, Mrs. Angeline
Kingsport, Miss Elizabeth
Knapp, Mrs. J. C.
Licht, Hon. George F.
Licht, Mr. Louis
Licht, Mrs. John
Lewis, Mrs. Florence
Lewis, Mr. Seth
Lewis, Mrs. Katherine
Lewis, Mr. and Mrs. Alfred G.
Lincoln, Miss Rowena
LaForce, Miss Ida
Highfall, Miss Henrietta
LaPorte, Mrs. John
Langdon, Miss
Lane, Mrs. Myrtle
Mallett, Mrs. Sarah D.
Malette, Mrs. A.
Malette, Miss Elizabeth
Malette, Mr. and Mrs. F. A.
Means, Mr. and Mrs. George S.
Mead, Miss Caroline
McCarr, Dr. and Mrs. Will
Miller, Mrs. E. S.
Miller, Miss A. F.
Miller, Mr. G. S. (Peterboro, N. Y.)
Muirhead, Prof. John
McKane, Mr. and Mrs. S. G.
McMullen, Mrs. Mary
Moberg, Miss Harriet (Canandaigua)
Meehan, Miss Pauline (Seneca Falls)
Myers, Mrs. S. M.
Miller, Mrs. Dudley (Syracuse, N. Y.)
Mills, Mr. T. K.
Middlewood, Mrs. Fannie J.
Middlewood, Mrs. James M. T.
Montoe, Mrs. E. J.
Moore, Mrs. David D.
Moore, Mrs. W. S.
Nash, Prof. and Mrs. F. P.
Nester, Mrs. S. K.
Nicholas, Mrs. P. N.
Nicholas, Mrs (Chicago, Ill.)
O'Brien, Mr. and Mrs. W. Smith
Organ, Mrs. E. S. H.
Palmer, Mrs. Ed. H.
Partridge, Mr. and Mrs. W. H.
Patterson, Mrs. J. D.
Page, Mrs. F. J.
Page, Mrs. J. Aug
Page, Mrs. Joel A.
Powers, Mrs. Iina

Predmore, Mrs. Geo. (Caywood, N. Y.)
Pomeroy, Mrs. C. E.
Palmateer, Mrs. Sam'l
Pierce, Mrs. Kate
Pierson, Mr. S. D.
Pierson, Mr. Job
Powell, Mrs. Nathaniel
Potter, Mr. and Mrs. F. F.
Rampe, Mr. and Mrs. Cecilia Meyering (Rochester, N. Y.)
Robinson, Mrs. Jennie
Rose, Mr. and Mrs. O. J. C.
Rose, Mr. and Mrs. Hugh
Reynolds, Mrs. H. G.
Koenke, Mrs. Beckman
Koenke, Mrs. J. K.
Richards, Miss Mary
Richardson, Mr. Don (Porto Rico)
Schonten, Miss L. M.
Stewardson, Mrs. Langdon C.
Smith, Miss M. A.
Smith, Mr. Theo. J.
Suydam, Mrs. H. I.
Smith, Mr. William
Smith, Mrs. N. C.
Skinner, Mrs. J. E. (Stanley, N. Y.)
Stark, Mrs. A. T.
Spengler, Dr. John
Spengler, Mrs. I., C.
Stebbins, Mr. J. J. H.
Smith, Mrs. Green (San Francisco, Cal.)
Schmidt, Prof. Nathaniel (Jerusalem, Syria)
Scott, Miss Annie
Sweet, Dr. A. A.
Schieffelin, Mrs. Carrie
Sigler, Mrs. L. F.
Sattler, Mr. and Mrs. William
Tucker, Mrs. F.
Talman, Miss R. F. (St. Paul, Minn.)
Tuttle, Mrs. H. H. H.
Ver Planck, Mr. S. H.
Van Slyke, Dr. and Mrs. L. L.
Van Houten, Mrs. E. B.
Watson, Mrs. David
Wheat, Mrs. Corydon
Wheat, Mr. and Mrs. H. A.
Willard, Hon. S. D.
Wanless, Mr. Richard
Weld, Mr. R. A.
Wheeler, Mrs. Carrie
Wehnes, Mr. Conrad
Wilkinson, Miss Bessie

(9)

A sampling of speakers for the meeting of the Geneva Political Equality Club includes Dr. Frederick H. Willis in 1899, who spoke on "The Alcott Family and their Friends." *Geneva Historical Society*

Associate Members.

President Langdon C. Stewardson
Mr. and Mrs. Chas. Vail
Prof. John Silver
Rev. John B. Hubbs
Dr. and Mrs. H. R. Moody
Miss Wadsworth
Miss Jessie Wadsworth
Mrs. F. P. Nester
Miss Hattie Pope
Miss Ethel S. Slosson

Miss Sarah Slosson
Mrs. H. L. Slosson
Miss J. L. VerPlanck
Miss Mary Webster
Mrs. Helen Webster
Mrs. F. D. Fuller
Mrs. M. E. Benedict
Mr. J. F. Hale
Mr. Ed. H. Palmer
Mrs. N. B. Remick

Number of members in Geneva, . . . 262
Number of signed suffragists in Ontario County, . . - 961

In Wyoming, Colorado, Utah and Idaho, women have full political rights.

Copies of this program on sale at Miss Scott's. Price 10 cents.

(10)

Musicians Who Have Assisted Us.

Miss Agnes Morgan
Mrs. Smith Harriman
Prof. Charles Rose
Mrs. Lida Coleman Spengler
Mrs. O. J. C. Rose
Mrs. W. A. Gracey
Miss Adelaide Fowle
Prof. Muirhead

Mrs. Clark Pomeroy
Mrs. Nellie Nares Partridge
Miss Sarah W. Slosson
Miss Agnes Beven Slosson
Mr. W. A. Gracey
Mrs. Curtiss
Mrs. Cecelia M. Rampe
Mr. Heinrich Jacobsen

Mrs. H. K. Clapp

Ladies' Chorus from Choral Society.

Mrs. VanSlyke
Mrs. Benedict
Mrs. Harman
Mrs. Hart
Miss Sill
Mrs. Covert
Mrs. Hallenbeck
Miss Hemiup
Miss Miller

Mrs. Deegan
Mrs. Baldridge
Miss Baldridge
Miss Greene
Mrs. Guildford
Mrs. Schieffelin
Mrs. Nicholas
Mrs. Rose
Mrs. Pomeroy

Mr. Pole's Orchestra

(11)

Program for 1904-1905.

✎

I   Monday, Nov. 28th, 8 P. M.   At the President's House, Hobart College.
       Hostess—Mrs. Langdon C. Stewardson.
       Speaker—Miss Arria Huntington.
       Subject—Woman's Clubs, What after?

II   Monday, Dec. 19th, 8 P. M.   At No. 41 High Street.
       Hostess—Mrs. Angeline Keyes.
       Reports from Auburn Convention Delegates — Mrs. Covert,
          Dr. Greene, Mrs. Partridge, Mrs. Hallenbeck, Mrs. Jones.

III   Monday, Jan. 30th, 8 P. M.   Meeting in Public Hall.
       Speaker—Mrs. Ballington Booth.*
       Subject—The Way Out.

IV   Monday, Feb. 27th, 8 P. M.   At No. 7 N. Genesee St.
       Hostess—Mrs. W. F. Humphrey.
       Topic—The Peace Movement.

V   Monday, March 27th, 8 P. M.   Meeting in Public Hall.
       Speaker—Mrs. Anna Garlin Spencer.*
       Subject—The Ethics of Political Equality.

VI   Monday, April 24th, 8 P. M.   At Mrs. Hemiup Haley's, 19 Genesee St.
       Annual Meeting and Election of Officers.

VII   Monday, May 29th, 4-7 P. M.   Piazza Party at Lochland.
       Hostess—Mrs. E. S. Miller.
       Speaker—Miss Alice Stone Blackwell.

————

   * Subject to change.

GENEVA HISTORICAL SOCIETY

frage Association, and a frequent presenter at legislative hearings. Libby was awarded the position of honorary president of GPEC at its inception. Some other political equality clubs were inaugurated due to Anne's work in the central New York communities of Phelps, Clifton Springs, and Honeoye.[22]

One of the projects that Libby managed during the 1897-1911 life of GPEC—to the great benefit of future researchers—was the compiling of seven large scrapbooks that chronicle the activities of the club. They present a priceless review of attitudes and accomplishments of the suffrage workers, and are available online through the Rare Book and Special Collections Division of the Library of Congress. Part of the work of making the scrapbooks was completed during Libby's relaxing summer days at Fossenvue.[23]

The general philosophy of the Geneva Political Equality Club was represented through its two leaders. Libby and Anne represented a democratic aristocracy hospitable to creative and intellectual thought that supported social reform. Anne said of herself, "In my own case both heredity and environment conspire to make me a thorough believer in political equality." She viewed herself as

"a fairly intelligent, wholly responsible member of the community [and] not willing to wait in silence under the continued disqualification of sex. The time has come when it is neither just nor expedient for women to be denied the ballot on no other ground than that they are women.... In our present... industrial and constructive age we should consider the ballot as a means of bringing about better conditions; a tool for the building of cities and states which are fit for the children of a nation."[24]

The intellectual climate at GPEC was so receptive that "Regardless of one's politics, few refused invitations to significant occasions at Lochland." Anne and Libby were especially concerned to offer equal opportunities to both sexes. "Our so-called woman's movement," said Anne,

"is for the benefit of the people—men, women, and children.... Neither men nor women alone are wise enough to determine the conditions under which we shall live; that demands a consensus of the best feeling, thought, and action of which both men and women are capable—working together."[25]

One practice that does seem incongruous today is that, in spite of Libby's and Anne's inter-sex, cooperative, and equitable perspective, they could not avoid the dominant cultural practice of the day that referred to women using a label that attached them to some man. For instance, "Chair<u>man</u> of the Industrial Committee <u>Mrs.</u> Langdon C. Stewardson" (emphasis added). Was she a "<u>man</u>?" And what was <u>her</u> name? This issue became a major concern of the resurgent women's rights movement in the 1960s, but was not yet in the scope of women in the 1890s.[26]

An interesting feature of GPEC is its spectrum of interests, which reflected the fact that its leaders considered all of life to be "women's issues." The organization had seven standing committees: Industrial Conditions, Young People's Work, Membership, Literature Distribution, School Suffrage, Peace, and Legislative Work. Libby and Anne were delegates to the International Peace Conference in Boston in 1904, and to the National Arbitration and Peace Congress in New York City in 1907. And regarding membership, GPEC was the fastest growing political equality club in New York State. By 1907, it had 362 members.[27]

Meetings of GPEC were held monthly from November through May. The meetings were held at various venues in the Geneva area, with the final gathering in May being an elaborate "Piazza Party" at Lochland. The piazza on the house at Lochland was enormous, spanning almost the full circumference of the building. The over two-hundred guests who usually attended the party were pleased not only with the scenery of the estate and the lake, but also with the decorations of yellow flowers and banners (the suffrage color), and, of course, the speakers.

A sampling of Piazza Party speakers includes Dr. Frederick H. Willis in 1899, who spoke on "The Alcott Family and their Friends;" Annis Ford Eastman in 1902, who spoke on her experience as a minister at the Congregational Church in Brookton, NY with "Woman's Place in State and Church;" Anne Fitzhugh Miller, who spoke on Ralph Waldo Emerson in 1903; Harriet May Mills, whose topic in 1904 was "Our Heritage;" and Anna Howard Shaw, president of the National American Woman Suffrage Association, who spoke in 1907 on "The Power of Incentive."

Miss Elizabeth Cook, of the graduating class of Cornell University, spoke at the 1908 meeting. According to a newspaper report, she gave her "prize address, 'Men, Women and Human Beings,' and Prof. Ernest Schoder [gave] an address, 'The Man in the Case.' Baritone and Tenor songs [were] sung by Messrs. Charles Meehan and George Pelzer. Refreshments [were] served on the piazza."[28]

Other notable speakers at the monthly GPEC meetings included British suffragist Emmeline Pankhurst, founder of the Woman's Social and

Political Union in Britain; Susan B. Anthony, who spoke on the political rights of women; Alice Stone Blackwell, editor of <u>Women's Journal</u> in Boston, who spoke on "Reasons for Extending Suffrage to Women;" and Carrie Chapman Catt, who spoke to an audience of over 500 in 1903 on "Woman and the State." Catt had founded such powerful organizations as the League of Women Voters and the International Alliance of Women.[29]

Certainly the quality of the speakers was impressive, and a testimony to the reputation, intent, and work of Libby and Anne Miller. A more complete list of GPEC speakers is attached. Libby was directly involved with all of the work of GPEC, but focused most of her attention on the hospitality of accommodating so many people—especially so many influential and powerful people. Her reputation as a hostess rested not only on the work of her historic family, but also on the base of her own learning and teaching. Visiting Lochland made people feel good about themselves, and satisfied that their passionate work on reform issues was receiving a worthwhile public hearing. The combination of Libby, Anne, and their home acted as a magnet for people and a forum for heralding attitudes and feelings about woman suffrage.

But the process of pursuing that goal involved a lot more than just an annual piazza party. There were organizations to manage, meetings to attend, legislative hearings to testify at, and bills to lobby for. Although the potential tedium of such work was high, the Millers plodded on with it for years. Libby usually attended and spoke at the annual meetings of the New York State Woman Suffrage Association. It met in Geneva again in 1907, with the normal hospitality offered at Lochland. Also in 1907, Anne was a delegate to the National American Woman Suffrage Convention in Chicago. Libby, now 85 years old, did not attend, but did receive a letter of appreciation for her life's work from that convention. She was one of the presiding officers at the 1908 Buffalo convention of that association, and hosted the 1910 convention of the Ontario County Woman Suffrage Association in Geneva. When she did not attend the NAWSA convention in Washington, D.C. in 1910, they sent to her a notice of thanks for her work as a "pioneer in suffrage work."[30]

Legislative work also occupied Libby and Anne at times. They sent letters and petitions to legislative bodies, and appeared before legislative

Speakers.

Names of those who have come from afar to speak in Geneva under
Suffrage Auspices.

Mrs. Elizabeth Cady Stanton,	On the Constitutional Convention.
Miss Susan B. Anthony,	Review of Progress
	" The Duty our Government owes its newly acquired Possessions."
Mrs. Lillie Devereux Blake,	"The Need of Woman's Influence in Politics."
Miss Alice Stone Blackwell,	" Reasons for Extending the Suffrage to Woman."
Mrs. Mariana W. Chapman,	Response to Address of Welcome.
Mrs. Mary Lewis Gannett,	" Suffrage a Duty."
Mrs. Mary Seymour Howell,	" Half a Century of Suffrage Agitation."
Miss Julia R. Jenny,	" Woman and the Ballot."
	" The Legal Status of Woman."
Miss Harriette A. Keyser,	" Woman and the Labor Movement."
Rev. Annis Ford Eastman,	" Woman's Right."
	" Woman's Place in Church and State."
Mrs. Mary E. Craigie,	" Patriotism."
Miss Harriett May Mills,	" Financial Support of the Movement."
	"Organization of a Political Equality Club in Geneva."
	" Progress Through Organization."
	" Organization."
	" Our Heritage."
Rev. Anna Howard Shaw,	" The Fate of Republics."
	" The Power of Incentive."
Mrs. Anna Botsford Comstock.	" Miss Van Rensselaer as School Commissioner in Cattaraugus County."
Mr. John N. Robertson of England,	" The Vote of Woman."
Mrs. Ellen Hardin Walworth,	" Washington and Lincoln " and " Five Lectures on Parliamentary Procedure."
Mr. Henry Blackwell,	" Woman Suffrage and the Home."
Miss Jane Slocum,	" The International Council of Women in London."
Dr. Frederick H. Willis,	" The Alcott Family."
Mrs. Harriot Stanton Blatch,	" Effect of War on the Economic Position of Women."
	" Woman Suffrage in England."
	" The Woman who Toils."
	" Peace."

LIBBY USUALLY ATTENDED AND SPOKE AT THE ANNUAL MEETINGS OF THE NEW YORK
STATE WOMAN SUFFRAGE ASSOCIATION. IT MET IN GENEVA AGAIN IN 1907, AT LOCH-
LAND.   *GENEVA HISTORICAL SOCIETY*

Miss Pauline Goldmark,	" The Consumer's League."
Mrs. Ballington Booth,	" Hope Halls."
Mrs. Glendower Evans,	" The Phillipine Question."
Mrs. W. A. Montgomery,	" Women as School Commissioners."
Mrs. Ella Hawley Crossett,	" Organization of Woman Suffrage in New York State."
	" Women's Colleges in Germany and the German Schools."
Miss Gail Laughlin,	A Problem in Mathematics.
Mrs. Fenwick Miller,	" The Woman of Today; Her Duties, Possibilities and Hopes."
Mrs. Percy Widdrington,	" Ideals of Citizenship."
Mrs. Charlotte Perkins Gilman,	" The Mother's World."
	" Why Women Should Want to Vote."
Rev. Marie Jenney,	A local experience.
Mrs. Florence Howe Hall,	Farce—" The Judgment of Minerva."
Mrs. Carrie Chapman Catt,	" Woman and the State."
Prof. Nathaniel Schmidt,	" The Value of Political Equality."
Mr. Charles Brodie Patterson,	"Health, Happiness and Character Building."
	" The New Thought Attitude Toward Equality for Men and Women.
Mrs. Florence Kelly,	" Child Labor."
Miss Mary Merritt Crawford,	Cornell University—Sage College Suffrage Club

❧

Some of our neighbors who have spoken before the Club.

Rev. Dr. Converse,	" Suffrage in Wyoming."
Mr. Smith O'Brien,	" In Favor of Suffrage."
Mr. M. F. Blaine,	" Address of Welcome to State Convention."
Mr. Charles Hemiup,	" Preparation for the Ballot."
Rev. Dr. Remick,	" The Commonweal with incidental reference to Equality."
Miss Anne F. Miller,	" Reasons for Organizing."
	" Report of State Convention at Hudson."
	" Report of National Convention at Washington."
Dr. W. H. Jordan,	" Methods to be avoided."
Mrs. C. A. Baldridge,	" Woman's Work in the W. C. T. U."
	Parliamentary Procedure.
	" Report of State Convention at Hornellsville."
	The True Basis of Political Representation.
Mrs. Maria R. Hemiup,	" Woman's Part in the Rise and Fall of Greece and Rome."

Mr. Conrad Wehnes,	Purchase of Official Buildings.
Mr. F. A. Malette,	"How Should Geneva Streets be Paved."
Mr. P. N. Nicholas,	"Our City Government."
	"Woman Suffrage a Success in Idaho."
	Miss Anthony's Trial.
Mr. W. A. Gracey,	"The True Basis of Representation."
	Purchase of Official Buildings.
Mrs. Martha Ives,	"Why Should Missions Teach Colored Girls in the South."
Prof. Noa,	"Ought Women to Sit in Jury Box and on Bench?"
	"Reply to Judge Mason's Anti-Suffrage Arguments."
Mr. O. J. C. Rose,	Question Box, Replied to.
	"The True Basis of Representation."
Mrs. Florence Lewis,	"Report on State Convention at Glens Falls."
Prof. F. P. Nash,	"True Basis of Political Representation."
Rev. G. C. Baner,	"Report of State Convention at Oswego."
	"The True Basis of Political Representation.'
Mrs. Frank Guilford,	Report of Hornellsville Convention.
Mr. S. H. Ver Planck,	Reminiscences of Susan B. Anthony and Mrs. E. Cady Stanton.
Prof. J. H. McDaniels,	"The Countrywomen of Sappho."
Mr. Steward Dey,	"Geneva Fire Department."
Mr. C. T. Church,	"Appropriation for Fire Department."
Mrs. Chas. Congdon,	Buffalo Convention.
Mr. Chas. Congdon,	Purchase of Local Official Buildings.
Mrs. Hemiup Haley,	Buffalo Convention.
Mr. Edward Cook,	Trial of Miss Anthony.

Mr. S. D. Willard, Rev. J. H. Ballou, Mrs. J. E. P. Butts, Rev. A. H. Broadway, Rev. Lansing Bailey, Dr. Caroline Hemuip Perkins, Mrs. Charles Leonard, Mrs. George Schell, Mrs. McMullen, Dr. F. A. Greene, Mr. H. A. Wheat and Mrs. Henry B. Graves have also taken part in the meetings.

What we ask is simply this,—what all other classes have asked before :   Leave it to woman to choose for herself her profession, her education and her sphere   .   .   .   The sphere of each man, of each woman, of each individual, is that sphere which he can, with the highest exercise of his powers, perfectly fill   .   .   All that woman asks through this movement is, to be allowed to prove what she can do; to prove it by liberty of choice, by liberty of action, the only means by which it can ever be settled how much and what she can do.— WENDELL PHILLIPS.

GENEVA HISTORICAL SOCIETY

committees in support of woman suffrage. Both were present in the New York State Senate Chamber on February 22, 1899 in support of a bill to enfranchise taxpayers; Anne testified before the New York State Judiciary Committee in 1899, and they both worked through the legislative committee of the New York State Woman's Suffrage Associations, which often met at Lochland. The Geneva Advertiser Gazette noted:

LIBBY IN 1907, WHEN SHE WAS 85. THAT SAME YEAR, ANNE WAS A DELEGATE TO THE NATIONAL AMERICAN WOMAN SUFFRAGE CONVENTION IN CHICAGO. LIBBY DID NOT ATTEND THE CHICAGO CONVENTION, BUT DID RECEIVE A LETTER OF APPRECIATION FOR HER LIFE'S WORK IN WOMEN'S RIGHTS ADVOCACY.
FROM THE NAWSA COLLECTION

"There are few women in all the... country who put up stronger..., more convincing arguments than does Miss Anne Fitzhugh Miller...."[31]

The goal of all this activity, of course, was to reform existing laws that prevented women from voting. As previously noted, only four states or territories allowed women to vote as of 1896. There was one early exception. The 1776 constitution of the colony of New Jersey granted voting rights "to all inhabitants of this Colony, of full age, who are worth fifty pounds...." This right was rescinded by later legislation, and voting was restricted to males.[32]

The campaign to secure woman suffrage was difficult for all those involved as they battled the built-in headwind of cultural bias against women.

Perhaps more than anyone else, Elizabeth Cady Stanton represented the quality of effort that it took to persist. In a letter to Libby, she described her burned-out condition while on a speaking tour in the "western" (at the time) state of Missouri.

> "[I must speak] sixty-one more times…; shake hands with sixty-one more committees, smile, try to look intelligent and interested in every-one who approaches me, while I… endeavor to affect a little spring and briskness in my gait." Libby must have had mixed emotions—compassion for her cousin who was going through the horror of western travel in 1879, and elation because she was not a part of that.[33]

What Libby was going through was also frustrating. A bill to remove the word "male" from section one, article two of the New York State Constitution was submitted to the state legislature every year for decades with no success. In 1911, the year that Libby died, it came out of committee for a floor vote for the first time since 1895. It was killed in the senate. In spite of there being 155 suffrage organizations in New York State with over 55,000 members, the state legislature would not hear them. A large number of women converged on Albany on February 24, 1909 to attend a suffrage hearing in the Assembly Chamber—to no avail. On one occasion that must have felt satisfying, Libby contributed $300 to the successful effort in the state of Washington in 1910 to adopt a constitutional amendment to grant to women the right of suffrage. Or—as Gerrit would have said—to protect for women their natural right to suffrage.[34]

New York State finally did adopt woman suffrage legislation on November 6, 1917, the first eastern state to do so, thereby enfranchising over two million women. The shame of this state—and of this nation—is that residents like Elizabeth Cady Stanton, Anne Fitzhugh Miller, and Elizabeth Smith Miller were never allowed to register to vote.

XV

Final Days

In line with her sincere commitment to keep one's social life in order, Libby wrote her will when she was forty-eight years old. Perhaps that was a wise move, as a 'long life' did not mean in 1871 what it means now; the average life expectancy of a U.S. resident in 1860 was 41.8 years. Libby had been concerned that if she died before Charles, their $8,000-per-year income might not be adequate for him to continue living at Lochland. That became moot when he died fifteen years before Libby. As she survived Charles, her estate was to be divided equally among her surviving children. Her estate was valued at $782,667.

When Charles died in February of 1896, his funeral was held at Lochland. Elizabeth Cady Stanton attended, noting that it was a colorful, and not a depressive, occasion. There was, she said,

> "no black anywhere. Cousin Lizzie and all the women of the family, dressed in their usual colors, sat in the parlors conversing quietly with the guests." Charles "was dressed in his habitual drab suit...."

Felix Adler gave a few "farewell words" at both the house and the cemetery. Adler was a respected professor of Hebrew and Oriental languages at Cornell University.

> "A fine span of Charley's own horses drew the hearse, and Rolando, his favorite saddle-horse, followed with empty saddle."[1]

After Charles' death, Libby became more active in the suffrage movement. The Geneva Political Equality Club emerged in 1897, and the Elizabeth Smith Miller Study Club in 1907. She planned a full five-month series of programs for the Study Class from January through May of 1909 focusing on the lives of great men and women, and on national problems and ideals. In 1906, the <u>Geneva Advertiser Gazette</u> wrote of her, "She is the sweetest old lady that ever lived, so kind-hearted, so womanly, so rare in all good deeds. Her home is one of quiet refinement, [and] in nice weather we see her down street nearly every day, with a kindly smile, a pleasant word for everybody." Her old age was glorified in a touching poem by her Geneva friend Elizabeth A. Rose:

> "Lo, where prismic colors blend to white,
> Where winter's fingers sift her crystal snows,
> Where old December's early sunset glows,
> A brave and sturdy blossom toward the light
> Lifts its new face to bring a dear delight,
>> The waxen petals of a Christmas rose,
>> Wistful sweet blossom of the year's sweet close,
> Lingering to grace the speeding season's flight."

To Elizabeth Rose, Libby seemed to personify the Christmas rose.[2]

By the spring of 1910, Libby was ill at home. Anne needed to be close to care for her, so she resigned as president of GPEC, but was reelected as president anyway. The annual Piazza Party was scheduled at Lochland for May 30, but Libby was not able to host it due to her declining health. The party took place at the nearby country club on June 6. The featured speaker was Max Eastman, a 1905 graduate of William Smith College who, in 1910, founded the Men's League for Woman Suffrage.

During 1910, Anne was unable to attend GPEC meetings due to Libby's health, and was replaced as its president by "Mrs. Charles S. Burrall." Anne did participate on May 6, 1911 in a suffrage parade in New York City sponsored by the Women's Political Union, a suffrage organization transplanted from England to the United States by Elizabeth Cady Stanton's daughter Harriot Stanton Blatch who had lived in London for twenty years before re-

LIBBY AT HOME, HER DRESS ADORNED WITH A CHRISTMAS ROSE FROM THE
BUSH SHE PLANTED NEAR THE HOUSE. THE ROSE SURVIVES IN THE GARDEN TO
THIS DAY (SEE PICTURE ON NEXT PAGE). TO HER FRIEND ELIZABETH ROSE FROM
GENEVA, LIBBY PERSONIFIED THE CHRISTMAS ROSE.   *AUTHOR'S COLLECTION*

turning to the United States in 1902. She took with her to the parade a banner honoring Elizabeth Smith Miller made by GPEC. Designed by Anne,
the banner featured a silver shield with a Christmas rose embroidered into
it. The back side was yellow and contained the dates significant to Libby's
life—1822—1848—1911. Anne carried this banner in the parade sixteen
days prior to Libby's death, and must have felt proud to have this last chance
to publicly honor her mother.[3]

Libby died, evidently of natural causes, at the age of 88 at Lochland on
May 22, 1911. I was unable to acquire a copy of her death certificate from

the Canandaigua City Clerk's office without a court order because I am not a member of her family. But that may not be important; we know that she was in declining health for about a year before she died. A comment in the Ontario County Times noted her "fine eyes glowing with the light of the strong spirit that nothing but Death could quench."[4]

Libby's funeral was held at Lochland. The service was conducted by Rev. Samuel Eastman, pastor of Park Church in Elmira and a dedicated women's rights supporter. Others who addressed the funeral gathering included Hobart College President Langdon C. Stewardson, Cornell University professor Nathaniel Schmidt, and women's rights and peace advocate Anna Garlin Spencer. The hymn "Still, Still With Thee" was sung by "Mr. Humphrey," a tenor soloist from Rochester, and residents of Miller House at William Smith College also offered a hymn.[5]

At the October 19-25, 1911 convention of the National American Woman Suffrage Association in Louisville, KY, "Memorial resolutions were adopted for prominent suffragists who had died during the year, among them... Elizabeth Smith Miller." On September 20, 1911, what would have been Libby's 89th birthday, the public drinking fountain that she funded was dedicated in Geneva. Two of the Miller family horses were the first to drink from it. Later that day, Anne delivered a speech in Geneva in support of suffragists. Nine months later on March 1, 1912, Anne died in Boston. Her estate, valued at $303,500, was willed to her brother, Gerrit Smith Miller.[6]

It seems a tragedy that neither Libby nor Anne lived to see and feel the social equity for which they fought for so long. Only five years later, they would have been able to vote in New York State. I wonder if the legislators who listened to their pleas ever felt any remorse.

AUTHOR'S COLLECTION

EPILOGUE

As I write this epilogue to Elizabeth Smith Miller's life, I am sitting in the Land Office on the Gerrit Smith Estate—now a National Historic Landmark. It's a cold March afternoon in 2015, and over a foot of snow still blankets the ground. In my imagination, I picture it to be a similar afternoon in 1825.

The small 20'x25' room is toasty-warm as Gerrit takes a log from the pile in the corner and puts it in the stove. His desk has a pile of papers on one corner, with others spread out around the pile. He sits down to continue his friendly conversation with three Native Americans of the Oneida tribe who reminisce about Peter—Gerrit's father who negotiated land deals with them 30 years ago.

In a flash of action the door swings open and three-year-old Elizabeth rushes in, plants her hands on her hips, "Father, why are you always working with papers!? Mom says she wants to talk with you this evening about going to church." She nods at the smiling trio, fumbles with one of the papers, and takes off her boots so that her cold feet can feel the warm brick floor. "Good," says Gerrit, "we'll see to that. Now I must talk with my friends." Elizabeth 'reboots' and leaves, waving at the horse and sleigh traveling along Peterboro Road.

As Libby grows up, she will meet other interesting people in this room. In 1833, she and her overactive cousin Elizabeth Cady play practical jokes on people in the home, romp with the family dog Frolic around the clematis vine in the East Garden, and then burst into the Land Office where Gerrit and his clerk Caleb Calkins sit clustered around two runaway former slaves who arrived about half an hour ago. The one called Cuffy has bloody feet from walking on the stony ground. Toby has no shirt. His back is scarred and one half of his left ear is gone. They look as if they are afraid of someone—maybe Libby. The two girls stand still with hands behind their backs and listen to tales of horrible abuse. Gerrit sends them to the house to get a shirt and some shoes.

In October of 1839, Gerrit talked with Libby and Elizabeth Cady in this room about runaway former slave Harriet Powell who was hiding from her pursuing owner Mr. Davenport on the third floor of the house. He took them to meet Harriet and hear her stories of abuse.

And when Libby and Charles moved back to Peterboro in 1845, she had not yet met John Brown and Frederick Douglass, but she would—right here where I sit.

John Brown arrived for the first time in April of 1848 to seek Gerrit's aid in carrying out violent acts against slavery. Douglass was here soon after Brown seeking financial aid for his radical antislavery newspaper. Harriet Tubman also met Libby here with seven runaway former slaves in tow. These folks were giants who molded American history by reweaving the fabric of social relationships. I wonder what Libby learned from them—certainly a perspective on life oriented toward human rights and compassion.

Today, we can feel the fruits of the legacy that Elizabeth Smith Miller left for us. Her dedication to the issue of dress reform attracted national attention to the high intensity of discrimination against women, and catapulted militant women's rights advocates like Elizabeth Cady Stanton and Susan B. Anthony into the national political arena. In the early 1980s, some women of Peterboro who were—and still are—concerned about the abuse of women launched the Elizabeth Smith Miller Project to pursue justice for women. They pooled resources to make bloomers, march in women's rights parades, and develop support networks for victims of domestic violence. Their "Historical Daze" in Peterboro raised funds to support their goals, and to organize a conference at which visiting scholars presented their research on child abuse, domestic violence, sexual harassment and other human rights issues.[1]

A New York State Historical Marker was installed on the site of Libby's Peterboro home on October 28, 1998 to recognize her efforts in the dress reform movement. And in 1987, our national government created Women's History Month to be celebrated in March of each year. We must ask, why did it take so long to recognize the value of women in American history? And, more importantly, why is there not a Men's History Month? And co-incidentally, why is there a Black History Month (February), and no White History Month?

The answers to these questions—as Libby would point out—rests in the source of the discrimination. Who is doing it? It is, of course, the people who do not need a special month to commemorate them because they are—and have been—in power over all American history. A White Male History Month, therefore, would not make much sense.

Additional pieces of Libby's legacy include the contemporary organization Liberty Resources that provides services for victims of domestic violence in Madison County; "Women's Voices Radio" (FM 88.3) in Syracuse airs issues that concern women; The New York Women's Equality Coalition lobbies the state legislature regarding bills for equal pay, workplace accommodations for pregnancy, sexual harassment, and other women's interests. In January of 2015, New York State Senator Diane Savino (D-Staten Island) noted, "We've started the season talking about women's rights.... That... I've never seen before. So it's cause for optimism.... And we've never gotten this type of movement from Republicans in the past." I can picture Libby and Anne sitting before that legislature lobbying in the 1890s. If they could see this "movement" today, they would surely display the mixed emotions of being pleased that legislators are listening, but angry because it took them another 120 years to care.[2]

July 19, 2007 marked the 159th anniversary of the first Women's Rights Convention organized in part by "Cousin Lib Stanton" in Seneca Falls, NY. On that day, U.S. Senator Hillary Rodham Clinton (D-NY), and Representative Louise M. Slaughter (D-NY-28) introduced to the national legislature the National Women's Rights History Project Act. This bill is "designed to provide Americans with the opportunity to learn more about the heroines who fought tirelessly to secure women's rights in the United States." Signed in 2009, one goal of this Act is to establish a women's history automobile trail through central New York that would link sites significant in the women's rights and woman suffrage movements.[3]

Also, Libby would be proud to know that the National Collaborative for Women's History Sites was established in 2001 to "support and promote the preservation and interpretation of sites and locales that bear witness to women's participation in American life." It would seem that every inch of ground in the country would be part of that effort.[4]

Some other physical representations of Libby's legacy include Miller House and Lochland. William Smith College constructed Miller House in the early 1900s to honor Elizabeth Smith Miller's efforts to support education for women. As a dormitory today, it houses 42 female students. Each room has cable and Internet access, and "The Women's Collective, a student-run organization that studies women's issues, is located in the basement of the building."[5]

Lochland, the elegant home of Greene Smith from 1865 to 1869, and of Elizabeth Smith Miller from 1869 to 1911, was sold to Edward M. Mills in 1912. Mills was a director of Buffalo Mines Ltd., a company involved in silver mining. In 1933 it became a school for children with disabilities, and is now a "residential setting for developmentally disabled adults." In a move that I feel sure would please Libby, the League of Women Voters now holds its annual dinner at Lochland.[6]

The subjective side of Libby's legacy is embedded in the social values practiced in this historic Land Office, and impressed into the minds of people who came here, even if only with minor business to conduct. The key concept involved was empathy, always expressed by Gerrit and his family through his favorite rule—The Golden Rule to treat others as you would prefer to be treated.

Libby's life exemplified empathy in action. Her early contact with oppressed people imprinted in her mind a concern with their plight—especially women—and she worked for decades to secure their natural rights, and their access to education.

Libby excelled in those chosen areas that she deemed to be most important: natural beauty, domestic order, and hospitality. One writer has commented, "To many she will remain the one perfect woman known in a lifetime—her beautiful face radiant with... a love that permeated every thought and word and deed, that made her perfectly ordered home a heaven of comfort and peace, her friendship an inspiration and her memory a benediction for the years to come." Another commented, "it is impossible to depict the charm of her personality, something as indefinable as the fragrance of a flower, which drew all hearts to her." "Virtue went forth from her, and... a glimpse of her was like the sight of [Mt.] Monadnock from a flat country."[7]

Because Libby's main concerns were aesthetic and practical, the reform ethos was not primary. She became expert at the domestic and hospitality tasks that she loved, and was content to be Anne's helper in women's rights reform work. Were she with us today, she would see the hypocrisy in our pride about human rights accomplishments. After slavery was abolished legally, southern states enacted "Jim Crow" legislation designed to keep African-Americans "in their place," and authors today point out that "Jim Crow" continues to work through police and penal institutions. I submit that today there is a "Jim Crow" for women hidden in the administrative leadership of religious, business, and educational institutions that Libby would see easily.[8]

We can only speculate about what Libby might do about it, but we can be sure that her lifelong commitment to equity among people, her ability to see beauty in peace and order, her perception of value in and empathy for everyone, and her pervasive power through quietness and understanding form a model for all of us to emulate.

ACKNOWLEDGMENTS

Sincere thanks are due to Donna Dorrance Burdick (Town of Smithfield Historian), Jody Luce (living historian who portrays Elizabeth Smith Miller), and Dorothy H. Willsey (President of the National Abolition Hall of Fame and Museum, and Director of the Gerrit Smith Estate National Historic Landmark – both located in Peterboro, New York) for the use of their accumulated materials on Elizabeth Smith Miller during the research process.

Also appreciated are the efforts of the people who manage the Gerrit Smith Papers at Syracuse University Bird Library, Department of Special Collections; The Smith-Miller Papers at the Geneva Historical Society; The Gerrit Smith and Smith Miller papers at the Madison County Historical Society; and the Smith Papers at the Peterboro Area Historical Museum.

Special thanks are due to Rosemary Plakas and her efforts to digitize and make available on-line the Library of Congress collection of seven scrapbooks compiled by Elizabeth Smith Miller and Anne Fitzhugh Miller that cover the activities of the Geneva Political Equality Club.

Notes

Abbreviations Used in Notes

GS Gerrit Smith

ACS Ann Carroll Fitzhugh Smith

ESM Elizabeth Smith Miller (referred to as ESM both before and after her 1843 marriage)

SU Syracuse University, Bird Library Department of Special Collections

MCHS Madison County Historical Society

PHS Peterboro Historical Society

GHS Geneva Historical Society

AFM Anne Fitzhugh Miller

HWS History of Woman Suffrage

Notes

Chapter 1—Birth and Childhood

1. <u>Livingston County Leader</u>, Sept. 25, 1955, GHS.

2. ACS to Peter Smith, March 12, 1823; ACS to GS, July 17, 1823; Nov. 30, 1824; Dec. 28, 1824, SU.

3. ACS to GS, Dec. 2, 1824; ACS to her sister Betty, June 14, 1825; ACS to GS, Sept. 12, 1825; GS to ACS, Dec. 19, 1824, SU.

4. ACS to GS, June 14, 1825; GS to ACS, Feb. 26, 1831; March 6,

1831; March 16, 1831; Sept 12, 1825, SU.

5. ACS to GS, March 6, 1826; June 3, 1829; ACS to Elizabeth Fitzhugh, Dec. 27, 1827, SU.

6. ACS to GS, March 30, 1831; Syracuse Daily Journal, June 2, 1911; ESM to GS, Jan. 31, 1835; ESM to Mrs. Harvey, Nov. 15, 1833, SU.

7. ACS to GS, Feb. 22, 1834; GS to ACS, April 29, 1832, SU.

8. ACS to GS, March 30, 1831; April 7, 1831; ACS to ESM, Jan. 16, 1834; ESM to GS, March 22, 1831, SU.

9. ACS to GS, Aug. 19, 1833; Feb. 13, 1834; ACS to GS, Sept. 5, 1835, SU.

10. ACS to GS, May 14, 1836; June 11, 1836, SU.

11. ACS to GS, Dec. 13, 1846; Dec. 17, 1836; Dec. 19, 1836; Dec. 23, 1836; Dec. 31, 1836, SU.

12. ACS to GS, Dec. 13, 1836; Dec. 23, 1836, SU.

13. ACS to GS, Dec. 19, 1836, SU.

14. ACS to GS, Dec. 31, 1836, SU.

15. For an extensive coverage of visitors to the Smith home, see Dann, Practical Dreamer, chapter 5.

16. Syracuse Journal, June 2, 1911.

17. GS to ACS, April 14, 1831; Chadwick; S. Higgins to ESM, Jan. 1, 1875, SU.

18. The Daily Graphic, March 8, 1875.

19. Sarah Forten to Elizabeth Whittier, Dec. 25, 1836 in Sterling.

20. Verse Book introduction; Verse Book, Nov. 21, 1860, SU.

21. GS to ACS, Dec. 26, 1836, SU.

Chapter 2—Education

1. GS to ACS, March 30, 1831; April 4, 1831, SU.

2. ESM to Peter Smith, April 25, 1834, SU.

3. Weekly Recorder, July, 1898; Peterboro Historical Society Newsletter, Feb., 2008; King to GS, June 27, 1836, SU.

4. ESM to ACS, Jan. 22, 1836; Feb. 9, 1836; GS to ESM, Feb. 15, 1836, SU.

5. James, 540; ACS to ESM, May 11, 1836; July 4, 1835; May 22, 1835; June 23, 1835, SU.

6. ACS to ESM, May 22, 1835; June 23, 1835, SU.

7. ACS to ESM, May 6, 1835; May 22, 1835, SU.

8. ACS to ESM, Sept. 28, 1835; Betsey Kelty to ESM, Oct. 10, 1835, SU.

9. ACS to ESM, Jan. 23, 1836; Dec. 24, 1839; Jan. 23, 1836, SU.

10. ESM to ACS, Feb. 27, 1836; ACS to ESM, July 31, 1835; Dec. 2, 1835; ESM to ACS, Feb. 9, 1836, SU.

11. ESM to ACS, May 24, 1836, SU.

12. ESM to ACS + GS, Aug. 24, 1836; ESM to Miss King, June 6, 1838; ACS to GS, May 2, 1836, SU.

13. ACS to GS, Nov. 12, 1839; Dec. 5, 1839, SU.

14. Aunt Betsey to ACS + ESM, Nov. 13, 1839, SU.

15. ACS to GS, Nov. 8, 1839; Dec. 5, 1839; Dec. 10, 1839, SU.

16. ACS to GS, Nov. 15, 1839; Nov. 25, 1839; Dec. 10, 1839, SU.

17. ACS to GS, Nov. 23, 1839; Dec. 10, 1839; GS to ACS, Nov. 24, 1839; Dec. 11, 1839, SU.

18. ACS to ESM, Jan. 18, 1840; Jan. 28, 1840; Feb. 18, 1840, SU.

19. ACS to ESM, Jan. 18, 1840; Dec. 24, 1839; Feb. 15, 1840; Feb. 17, 1840; Feb. 20, 1840; Feb. 28, 1840, SU.

20. ACS to ESM, Feb. 24, 1840; Feb. 18, 1840; Jan. 18, 1840; Feb. 24, 1840, SU.

21. ACS to ESM, March 3, 1840; Jan. 30, 1840; Feb. 11, 1840, SU.

22. ESM to GS, March 20, 1860; Feb. 2, 1861; March 18, 1861; Jan. 20, 1869, SU.

Chapter 3—Health Issues

1. ACS to GS, Oct. 2, 1846; ACS to ESM, June 7, 1852; ACS to GS, June, 1833, SU.

2. ACS to GS, Jan. 22, 1825; Jan. 2, 1837; ACS to Peter Smith, Jan. 9, 1837; GS to ACS, April 3, 1831; ESM to GS, Sept. 13, 1836; ACS to ESM, June 25, 1845, SU.

3. ESM to GS, Oct. 3, 1844; Oct. 5, 1844; Feb. 4, 1845, SU.

4. ACS to ESM, March, 1845, SU; email, John Bowen, MD to Norman Dann, Feb. 21, 2015.

Chapter 4—Marriage and Income

1. Common Place Book, SU.

2. ACS to ESM, Oct. 28, 1843; Nov. 14, 1843, SU; Miller.

3. Sherman, 9; GS to ACS, Aug. 20, 1843, SU.

4. Madison County Eagle, Oct. 25, 1843; Elizabeth Kelty to Caroline King, Nov. 25, 1843, PHS.

5. Kelty to King, Nov. 25, 1843, PHS; GS to ESM, Sept. 23, 1843; GS to CDM + ESM, Oct. 18, 1843; ACS to ESM, Oct. 26, 1843, SU.

6. Scrapbook 7, 152.

7. Madison County Whig, April 29, 1846; June 10, 1846; CDM to GS, Dec. 23, 1846; GS to CDM, Dec. 13, 1862, SU.

8. Greene Smith to GS, July 28, 1869; CDM to GS, April 23, 1862, SU.

9. ACS to ESM, Dec. 7, 1843; Betsey Kelty to Caroline King, Nov. 25, 1843, SU.

10. Blatch, "Addresses".

11. Geneva Gazette, Feb. 7, 1896; The News Letter, Feb. 15, 1896.

12. Verse Book, 35, 129, SU; Geneva Gazette, Feb. 7, 1896.

13. ACS to ESM, Jan. 4, 1845; June 11, 1845; ESM to GS, Feb. 11, 1874, SU.

14. Common Place Book; Syracuse Herald American, March 1, 1998.

15. ACS to ESM, Dec. 7, 1843; Feb., 1845, SU; Kelty to King, Nov. 25, 1843, PHS.

16. ACS to ESM, March, 1845; Jan. 25, 1844; April 10, 1845, SU.

17. ESM to CDM, no day, 1846, SU.

18. Verse Book; ESM to CDM, Jan. 30, 1861; ACS to ESM, Dec. 14, 1864, SU.

19. Verse Book, SU.

20. Huntsinger, 97.

21. CDM to GS, May 2, 1862; ACS to ESM, Oct. 15, 1845, SU.

22. GS to ESM, Dec. 13, 1864; ESM to GS, Oct. 27, 1870; ESM to GS, March 24, 1871; Aug. 31, 1871, SU.

23. GS receipts; Common Place Book; ESM to GS, Mach 6, 1861, SU; Oneida Sachem, April 24, 1858.

24. GS to ESM, Dec. 13, 1864; ESM to GS, Nov. 9, 1872, SU.

25. ESM to GS, Aug. 14, 1870; March 23, 1871; April 13, 1872; June 8, 1874, SU.

26. Verse Book, SU.

Chapter 5—Early Residences

1. ACS to ESM, April 6, 1844; Feb., 1845; March, 1845; GS to ACS, Dec. 29, 1844; GS to ESM + CDM, March 1, 1845, SU.
2. GS to ESM + CDM, March 1, 1845, SU.
3. ACS to ESM, March, 1845; GS to John B. Mullin, April 14, 1846, SU.
4. U.S. Census, 1850.
5. ESM to ACS, Oct. 20, 1852, SU.
6. Verse Book, SU; Frothingham, 213.
7. Harlow, 314-318.
8. Ibid., 319.
9. Day Book; ESM diary, 1856, MCHS; ACS to ESM, April 6, 1865, SU; ESM journal, MCHS.
10. ESM to GS, March 17, 1863, SU.

Chapter 6—Children

1. ACS to ESM, Jan., 1845, SU.
2. ACS to ESM, Feb. 4, 1845; Aunt M. to ACS, Feb. 5, 1845, SU.
3. ACS to ESM, Feb., 1845; Betsey Kelty to ESM, Feb., 1845, SU.
4. ACS to ESM, March 7, 1845, SU.
5. ACS to ESM, May 30, 1845, SU.
6. ACS to ESM, July 17, 1846; ESM to ACS, Dec. 19, 1846, SU; ECS to ESM, April 15, 1847 in Gordon.
7. ACS to ESM, Sept. 14, 1851; Oct. 20, 1851, SU.
8. Elizabeth Cady Stanton to ESM, May 10, 1863 in Gordon, 486-487.
9. Sernett, 18FF; ACS to ESM, Nov. 3, 1870, SU.
10. Sarah M. Grimké to ESM, Sept. 14, 1850; ESM to GS, Nov. 28, 1861; E.C. Stanton to ESM, May 10, 1863; ACS to ESM, Jan. 4, 1858, SU.
11. C.D. Miller II to GS, March 3, 1867; March 6, 1868; Nov. 14, 1869; Aug. 28, 1871, SU.
12. C.D. Miller II to GS, Nov. 8, 1870; Dec. 6, 7, 1871; July 11, 1873; C.D. Miller II to ESM, Oct. 26, 1874, SU; Oswego Daily Times, Oct. 8, 1894.
13. Sarah Grimké to ESM, Sept. 14, 1850, PHS.
14. ESM to GS, no day, 1874, SU.
15. Verse Book, SU; ESM journal, MCHS.
16. ACS to GS, June 5, 1863; ACS and Nannie Miller to ESM, no day,

1863; ACS to ESM, Nov. 12, 1863, SU.

17. <u>Poultry World</u>, 1873; ESM to GS, July 27, 1870; ACS to ESM, Oct. 18, 1870; Oct. 15, 1870, SU.

18. ACS to ESM, Nov. 2, 1871; W.F. Miller to GS, 1873; ACS to ESM, Feb. 6, 1873, SU.

19. ESM to GS, no day, 1874, SU.

20. ESM journal, MCHS; ACS to ESM, March 10, 1856, SU.

21. ESM journal, MCHS.

22. <u>Ibid</u>., poem July 24, 1857.

23. ESM journal, MCHS.

24. Verse Book, SU.

25. ESM to GS, March 19, 1867; Feb. 18, 1868; Feb. 24, 1868, SU; ESM journal, MCHS.

26. ESM to GS, Feb. 24, 1868, SU; ESM journal, MCHS.

27. GS to ACS, Dec. 18, 1861; Jan. 2, 1862; Dec. 24, 1861, SU.

28. ESM journal, MCHS; ESM to Aunt Mary, May 2, 1862; Poem, March 4, 1862, SU.

29. ACS to ESM, June 5, 1867; Jan. 6, 1872; ESM to GS, April 2, 1870; AFM to GS, April 27, 1868, SU.

30. Huff, 327; Family Search document; ESM to GS, June 17, 1873, SU.

31. ESM to GS, April 28, 1868; May 3, 1868, SU.

Chapter 7—Religion

1. ACS to ESM, Feb. 22, 1836, SU.

2. ESM to GS, Feb. 27, 1836; Aug. 24, 1836, SU.

3. GS to ACS, May 1, 1836, SU.

4. ACS to ESM, May 27, 1836; June 11, 1836; May 21, 1839; Common Place Book, SU.

5. ACS to ESM + CDM, Dec. 7, 1843; ACS to ESM, Jan. no day, 1845; GS to ACS, Jan. 2, 1844, SU.

6. ACS to ESM, Oct. 27, 1845; Sarah M. Grimké to ESM, Sept. 14, 1850, SU.

7. Verse Book; Elizabeth Cady Stanton to ESM, April 20, 1850, SU.

8. ESM to GS, no day, 1861; Verse Book; ESM to GS, Aug. 21, 1867, SU; ESM to Elizabeth Cady Stanton, Sept. 2, 1886 in Gordon, vol. IV.

Chapter 8—Personal Interests

1. ACS to ESM, winter, 1844; Feb. 12, 1872; Jan. 4, 1845; March 14, 1865; Jan. 20, 1865; Aug. 15, 1845, SU.
2. Verse Book, SU.
3. T. Stanton, vol. 2 in note, 31, 32; Elizabeth Cady Stanton to ESM, Aug. 13, 1865 in T. Stanton, vol. 2, 106.
4. ECS to ESM, Oct. 22, 1866; July 20, 1839; Feb. 11, 1851 in T. Stanton, vol. 2, 114-115, 4, 26.
5. ESM to GS, no day, 1861; May 4, 1862, MCHS; ACS to ESM, April 18, 1865; June 14, 1868, SU.
6. ACS to ESM, Nov. 13, 1843, SU.
7. Day Book; ACS to ESM, June 4, 1873; March 3, 1840, SU.
8. ACS to ESM, Jan. 18, 1840; Jan. 13, 1844; Dec. 1, 1843, SU.
9. F.M. Haight to GS, Jan. 9, 1823, SU.
10. Verse Book, SU.
11. Common Place Book, SU.
12. GS to ACS, May 26, 1854; ACS to ESM, Oct. 12, 1861; Verse Book, 136, SU.
13. Verse Book, 150; ESM to GS, March 7, 1872; March 19, 1867; Aug. 21, 1867; ESM to ACS, Dec. 19, 1846; ESM to GS, Sept. 13, 1842, SU.
14. ESM to GS, March 6, 1868; Aug. 22, 1874; Sept. 2, 1874; Dec. 3, 1874, SU.
15. ACS to ESM, Sept. 19, 1873; Sept. 20, 1852; ACS to GS, Aug. 13, 1838; Verse Book, 85, SU.
16. ACS to GS, Jan. 23, 1850; ACS to ESM, no date; ESM to GS, March 23, 1873; April 18, 1873; ACS to GS, March 26, 1873, SU.
17. ACS to ESM, June 11, 1871; Sept. 19, 1873; ACS to GS, April 10, 1873, SU.
18. ACS to ESM, Nov. 7, 1870; ESM to the Cochrans, no day, 1875, SU.
19. Dann, Greene....
20. Day Lily, vol. 1, no. 3, 1983; www.campus.hws.edu/nfw/pss/scrap.html; Blatch, American....
21. The World, Jan. 3, 1895; Plakas.
22. GS to ESM, Nov. 14, 1843; ACS to ESM, Jan. 17, 1844, SU.

23. Common Place Book, SU; Stanton, 345; ACS to ESM, Feb. 12, 1844, SU.

24. ESM + GS to ACS, Sept. 3, 1842; Edwin Morton, Verse.

25. ECS to ESM, June 4, 1839, SU.

26. Geneva Gazette, 1875; Huff, "Elizabeth...."

27. www.radcliffe.harvard.edu.

28. Miller, In...., 24, 282-283, 23.

29. ESM to GS, no day, 1874; ECS to ESM, Dec. 16, 1874 in T. Stanton, vol. 2, 146; ESM to GS, no day, 1874, SU.

30. ESM to GS, Oct. 26, 1874; ACS to Greene and Bess, Oct. 12, 1873, SU.

31. ACS to ESM, Nov. 9, 1874; ESM to GS, Aug. 25, 1874, SU.

32. Miller, In..., 17-19.

33. Ibid., 20-23.

34. Ibid., 21-22.

35. Ibid., 99.

36. Ibid., 27-29, 67, 333.

37. Ibid., 547, 19, 124.

38. Ibid., 5, 29-30.

39. Ibid., 499; recipe pages listed in text.

40. Ibid., 433, 279-281, 520; ESM to GS, March 31, 1874; ACS to ESM, Feb. 3, 24, 1874, SU.

41. Miller, In..., 548-552, 25-27, 540-558, 570, 529-531, 563-564, 53-54.

42. Miller, In..., 23.

43. ACS to ESM, Nov. 21, 1864; Aug. 23, 1870; April 26, 1868; Elizabeth Cady Stanton to ESM, June 4, 1839; April 20, 1850; ESM to GS, Oct. 6, 1842, SU.

44. Day Book; Common Place Book, SU.

45. ACS to ESM, Oct. 27, 1845; Common Place Book; Day Book; ACS to GS, Dec. 22, 1859, SU; Blatch, American....

46. Day Book; Common Place Book, SU; Oswego Palladium, Dec. 11, 1890.

Chapter 9—Travel

1. ESM to GS, Aug. 11, 1841, SU.

2. ESM to GS, Feb. 27, 1861, SU.

3. Dann, <u>Practical</u>...., ix.

4. ACS to GS, April 12, 1844; Sept. 6, 1868; Feb. 18, 1863, SU.

5. ACS to GS, Oct. 30, 1861; ESM to GS, May 4, 11, 1861, SU.

6. ESM to GS, Nov. 27, 1861; Verse Book, SU.

7. ESM to GS, Nov. 29, 1861; Dec. 14, 1861, SU.

8. ESM to GS, Jan. 5, 1862; CDM to GS, Jan. 5, 1862, SU.

9. ACS to GS, Feb. 29, 1862; March 6, 1862; ESM to GS, March 3, 1862; Feb. 14, 1862, SU.

10. ACS to GS, March 16, 1862; ESM to GS, Feb. 22, 1862; March 30, 1862, SU.

11. ESM, to GS, April 6, 1862; April 20, 1862; April 23, 1862; May 16, 1862; ACS to GS, April 27, 1862, SU.

12. ESM to GS, May 11, 1862, SU.

13. ESM to GS, no day, 1862, SU.

Chapter 10—Lochland

1. Bessie to ACS, April 13, 1865; Greene Smith to ACS, April 13, 1865; Greene Smith to GS, May 8, 1865, PHS.

2. Greene Smith to ACS, June 17, 1865, PHS; Greene Smith to GS, Jan. 3, 1868, SU.

3. <u>Geneva Gazette</u>, Oct. 30, 1868; Greene Smith to GS, Feb. 6, 1868; ESM to GS, Jan. 14, 1869; Sept. 9, 1868, SU; ESM journal, MCHS.

4. ESM journal, MCHS.

5. GS to ESM, July 16, 1869, SU.

6. ESM to GS, July 21, 1869; July 27, 1869, SU.

7. ESM to GS, Sept. 30, 1869; Oct. 21, 1869; Dec. 19, 1869, SU.

8. <u>The Woman's Journal</u>, Nov. 3, 1897, GHS; ESM to GS, Oct. 21, 1869; ESM to ACS, Sept. 15, 1869, SU; conversation with Dorothy Willsey, March 4, 2015.

9. ESM to Bess, March 3, 1876; ESM to GS, March 7, 1872; April 26, 1874; March 31, 1874; July 1, 1874; July 6, 1874; ESM to Bess, Aug. 28, 1881, SU.

10. ESM to GS, no day, 1874; June 18, 1869; Sept. 7, 1869; ACS to ESM, June 12, 1870, SU; Blatch, <u>American</u>...., 310.

11. Scrapbook 9, 5; Huff, <u>Elizabeth</u>..., 4; <u>Ontario County Times</u>, Feb. 21,

1917; ECS note at Lochland, April 12, 1894; www.winningthevote.org/ AFMiller.html.

12. ESM to Bess, July 23, 1885; Verse Book, 345; ACS to ESM, Nov. 22, 1871; Greene Smith to GS, June 18, 1875; ESM to GS, Nov., 1874; William Fitzhugh Miller to   GS, Nov. 13, 1874, SU.

13. Marshall, 92-93.

Chapter 11—Fossenvue

1. Fossenvue, 5.

2. Leakey, 10.

3. Fossenvue, 143, 216.

4. Ibid., 233-240; Fossenvue Journal, 1908.

5. Fossenvue, opposite 112.

6. Ibid., 70, 56, 98; Fossenvue Journal, 1908.

7. Fossenvue, 59, 155.

8. Madison Scene, Sept. 15, 2004; Fossenvue, 23-24; Zogg.

9. Sarah W. Slosson to AFM, July 30, 1908 in Fossenvue Journal, 1908; Fossenvue, 185; Zogg.

10. Fossenvue Journal, 1908; Zogg.

11. Fossenvue Journal, 1908; Dann, Greene....

12. Fossenvue Journal, 1908; Fossenvue, 150, 141.

13, Fossenvue, 114.

14. Zogg.

15. Fossenvue; Green Mountain... Notes, 1-2.

Chapter 12—Philanthropy

1. ACS to GS, Dec. 9, 1859; ESM to ACS, Feb. 27, 1836, SU.

2. Common Place Book; ACS to ESM, July 20, 1871, SU.

3. Scrapbook 9, 5.

4. Syracuse Herald, May 24, 1911; Geneva Advertiser, March 7, 1893; clipping, GHS; ESM to GS, Jan., 1869, SU.

5. ACS to GS, Nov. 23, 1839, SU; www.winningthevote.org/AFMiller. html.

6. Day Book; ESM to GS, Aug. 11, 1841, SU.

7. Scrapbook 7, 153; Geneva Times, Dec. 23, 1963.

8. Smith, Warren, 191, 192, 197; www.hws.edu/New/pss.scrap.html.

9. Finger Lakes Times, May 2, 1909.

10. Peter Skenandoah Smith to ACS, June 16, 1836; Verse Book, 175-176, SU.

11. Elizabeth Cady to GS, Jan. 31, 1835; ESM to GS, May 16, 1836; Feb. 6, 1837, SU.

12. ESM to Wilbur H. Siebert, Sept. 2, 1896; ACS to GS, Nov. 12, 1839; ACS to ESM, Feb. 7, 1840; ACS to GS, June 5, 1863; ESM to GS, June 8, 1863; ECS to ESM, Nov. 21, 1852; July 20, 1863, SU.

13. GS to ACS, Aug. 20, 1843, SU.

14. The Standard, May 31, 1877.

15. ESM to Greene Smith, May 24, 1875; O.B. Frothingham to Greene Smith, April 10, 1875, SU.

16. O.B. Frothingham to Greene Smith, Aug. 29, 1876, SU.

17. Greene Smith to GSM, Jan. 7, 1878; ESM to Greene Smith, Jan. 8, 1878, SU; New York Herald, Feb. 21, 1878.

18. Harlow, 53.

19. Greene Smith to GSM, Jan. 7, 1878, SU; Utica Morning Herald, March 8, 1878.

20. ESM to Greene Smith, March 10, 1878; Greene Smith to ESM, March 14, 1878; ESM to Greene Smith, March 20, 1878; Greene Smith to GSM, March 26, 1878, SU.

21. Greene Smith to GSM, March 26, 1878; April 9, 1878; Greene Smith to ESM, June 2, 1878, SU.

22. ESM to Greene Smith, March 28, 1878, SU.

23. ESM to Greene Smith, March 30, 1878; G. P. Putnam's Sons to H. K. Armstrong, April 9, 1878; ESM to Greene Smith, April 14, 1878; ESM to Greene Smith, Oct. 11, 1878; ESM to Bessie, Nov. 5, 1878; G.S. Miller to Greene Smith, Feb. 14, 1878, SU.

Chapter 13—Dress Reform

1. History of Woman Suffrage, vol. I, 13.

2. The Lily, March, 1851.

3. Kesselman, 496, 498; GS to Elizabeth Cady Stanton, Dec. 1, 1855, SU; Nies, 63; ESM to Miss King, Jan. 6, 1838, SU.

4. Jackson in Woolson, 68-69.

5. Woolson, 134; The Lily, Jan., 1852; Bloomer, D.C., 71.

6. Bloomer, D.C., 67-68.

7. http://libwww.syr.edu/digital/exhibits/g/GerritSmith/esm.htm

8. Curtis, 12; Catherine Smith, 27-28; Kesselman, 497.

9. Harper, 114.

10. The Lily, June, 1851; The Sibyl, Oct. 1, 1857; Riegel, "Women's Clothes...," 397.

11. Woolson, 171; The Lily, March, 1851.

12. Brooklyn Eagle, Jan. 14, 1857.

13. The Sibyl, July, 1857; Sept. 1, 1856; GS to Elizabeth Cady Stanton, Dec. 1, 1855, SU.

14. Stafford in Woolson, 16-21.

15. Griffith, 71; Stafford in Woolson, 23.

16. The Lily, June, 1851; Jan., 1852.

17. Woolson, 135, 175.

18. Scrapbook 7, 52.

19. Williard, no page; Jackson in Woolson, 69.

20. Riegel, "Women's Clothes...," 398; The Lily, Feb., 1851.

21. GS to the Dress Reform Association, May 18, 1857, SU.

22. History of Woman Suffrage, vol. 1, 469-471; Fitzhugh, 131-132.

23. Beale, 58-61.

24. Syracuse Daily Courier, June 18, 1857; New York Times, Oct. 15, 1852; Jan. 31, 1852; International Monthly, Nov., 1851.

25. Brooklyn Eagle, Feb. 17, 1853; Elizabeth Cady Stanton to ESM, June 4, 1851 in T. Stanton, vol. 2, 29, 31; The Lily, Aug., 1852.

26. New York Times, Oct. 1, 1851; Sept. 7, 1876; The Illustrated London Times, Sept. 13, 1851; Woolson, 141.

27. Verse Book, 54, SU.

28. The National Era, Aug. 31, 1854; ACS to GS, May 18, 1851, SU; Buffalo Republic, Nov., 1851.

29. Arena, Sept., 1892.

30. The Lily, Aug., 1852.

31. The World, Jan. 13, 1895; Cunningham, 41, 65.

32. The World, Jan. 13, 1895; The Sibyl, Sept. 9, 1856.

33. Printed in The Lily, April, 1851.

34. The Lily, Feb., 1851.

35. The Sibyl, Feb., 1857; ECS to ESM, Aug. 5, 1851 in T. Stanton, vol. 2, 34.

36. Elizabeth Cady Stanton to Henry B. Stanton, April 11, 1851; Aug. 5, 1851; Oct. 18, 1851 in T. Stanton, vol. 2, 27, 37; The Lily, April, 1852.

37. Elizabeth Cady Stanton to ESM, May 1, 1853 in T. Stanton, vol. 2, 50.

38. Riegel, "Women's Clothes...," 390; The Sibyl, Jan. 15, 1857; Syracuse Daily Courier, June 18, 1857.

39. Verse Book, 56-57, SU; Fredonia Censor, June 17, 1851.

40. Brooklyn Eagle, Aug. 18, 1851.

41. A. Bloomer in Religio-Philosophical Journal; Kesselman, 500; Harper, 117.

42. Elizabeth Cady Stanton to ESM, May 1, 1853; June 13, 1853; Stanton to Susan B. Anthony, Sept. 10, 1855 in T. Stanton, vol. 2, 59, 50.

43. Curtis, 13; Blatch, 308; Common Place Book, clipping from "Evening Bulletin," July 1, 1851, SU.

44. James; http://libwww.syr.edu/digital/exhibits/g/GerritSmith/esm.htm.

45. Annual Report of the Oneida Association, 1849; Fischer, 240-265.

46. Gordon, vol. 2, 254; www.winningthevote.org/ESMiller.html.

47. The World, Jan. 13, 1895; Madison Observer, Sept. 16, 1868; Stauffer, 215; Oneida Dispatch, Aug. 21, 1868; Rochester Evening Express, Sept. 8, 1868.

48. Philadelphia Inquirer, Aug. 29, 1892; Day Lily, vol. 1, no. 2, 1983.

49. Syracuse Herald American, March 26, 2000.

Chapter 14—Political Interests

1. Huff, "The...," 7.

2. HWS, I, 472.

3. Huff, "Anne...," 345-348.

4. Preston.

5. Elizabeth Cady Stanton to ESM, Nov. 15, 1856; Sept. 20, 1855 in T. Stanton, vol. 2, 68-69; ACS to GS, May 1, 1858, SU.

6. Plakas speech in Peterboro; www.wwhp.org/Resources/Woman'sRights/

call.html.

7. <u>HWS</u>, IV, 435; <u>Syracuse Journal</u>, June 2, 1911; ESM to GS, Jan. 14, 1869; March 28, 1869, SU.

8. www.winningthevote.org/ESMiller.html; memory....; <u>Auburn Weekly Bulletin</u>, April 19, 1894; Gordon, vol. II, 133; <u>HWS</u>, V, 59-60.

9. ESM to GS, May 8, 1837, SU; memory....

10. Kotary, 9; Elizabeth Cady Stanton to ESM, Jan. 23, 1877, SU.

11. memory..., Elizabeth Cady Stanton to ESM, June 25, 1871 in T. Stanton, vol. 2, 134-135.

12. memory..., www.hws.edu/New/pss/scrap.html; Elizabeth Cady Stanton to ESM, Aug. 10, 1870 in T. Stanton, vol. 2, 128.

13. <u>Syracuse Post Standard</u>, Jan. 4, 1908; memory...; Huff, "Anne...."

14. Gordon, vol. 2, 193.

15. memory...; www.hws.edu/New/pss/coleburn.html

16. <u>New York Times</u>, April 13, 1853.

17. Thomas Mott Osborne to AFM, May 6, 1907 in memory....

18. Kotary, 10.

19. Dann, <u>Cousins</u>..., 169, 179, 198.

20. memory....

21. <u>HWS</u>, IV, 844; memory....

22.   memory...;   www.campus.hws.edu/New/pss/scrap.html;   Huff, "Anne...," 326; <u>Ontario County Times</u>, Feb. 21, 1917.

23. http://memory.loc.gov/ammem/collections/suffrage/millerscrapbooks/essay.html; Fossenvue Journal, 1908.

24. <u>The Geneva News</u>, Jan. 20, 1910.

25. www.campus.hws.edu/New/pss/scrap.html.

26. memory....

27. Huff, "Anne...," 330, 334; memory...; membership list compliments of GHS.

28. GPEC program compliments of GHS; memory...; <u>Geneva Advertiser Gazette</u>, May 28, 1908.

29. Huff, "Anne...," 339-340; memory....

30. <u>The Syracuse Post Standard</u>, Oct. 15, 1906; <u>HWS</u>, VI, 443; <u>HWS</u>, V, 208-209, 288; memory....

31. <u>HWS</u>, IV, 861; <u>Geneva Advertiser Gazette</u>, March 22, 1906; <u>Geneva</u>

Daily Times, Oct. 31, 1906.

32. Wellman, 138.

33. Elizabeth Cady Stanton to ESM, March 26, 1879 in T. Stanton, vol. 2.

34. memory...; HWS, VI, 673, 682.

Chapter 15—Final Days

1. ESM to GS, March 16, 1871, SU; Elizabeth Cady Stanton diary, Feb. 9, 1896 in T. Stanton, vol. 2; Geneva Advertiser Gazette, March 14, 1912.

2. Geneva Advertiser Gazette, Oct. 25, 1906; Poem, GHS.

3. memory...; Plakas speech, 20.

4. memory...; Ontario County Times, Feb. 21, 1917, and in Day Lily, vol. 1, no. 3, 1983.

5. Scrapbook 9, undated clipping, 5.

6. HWS, V, 328; Huff, "Anne...," 327; Syracuse Herald, May 27, 1911.

Epilogue

1. Day Lily, vol. 1, 1983; Oneida Daily Dispatch, July 20, 1981; July 23, 1982; Day Lily, vol. 1, no. 6, 1983.

2. www.LibertyResources.org; Syracuse Post Standard, Sept. 3, 2007; Oneida Daily Dispatch, Jan. 18, 2015.

3. Women in Motion, Sept. 2007; f\v10\071107\071107.299.xml.

4. www.NCWHS.org.

5. www.hws.edu.

6. Madison County Leader and Observer, July 25, 1912; www.Lochland-inc.org; email, Deb Kraft, director of Lochland School to Dot Willsey, May 20, 2009.

7. http://home.comcast.net/~madisoncounty/roots/ MillerElizabethSmith.htm; memory....

8. Alexander.

BIBLIOGRAPHY

BOOKS

Alexander, Michelle. <u>The New Jim Crow</u>, New York: the New Press, 2012.

Beale, Irene A. <u>Genesee Valley Women</u>, Geneseo, NY: Chestnut Hill Press, n.d.

Blackwell, Alice Stone. <u>Lucy Stone: Pioneer of Woman's Rights</u>, University of Virginia Press, 1930.

Bloomer, D.C. <u>Life and Writings of Amelia Bloomer</u>, Boston: Arena Publishing Company, 1895.

Chadwick, John White, ed. <u>A Life for Liberty: Anti-Slavery and Other Letters of Sallie Holley, 1818-1893</u>, New York: G.P. Putnam's Sons, 1899.

Clinton, Catherine. <u>Harriet Tubman: The Road to Freedom</u>, New York: Little, Brown and Company, 2004.

Cunningham, Patricia. <u>Reforming Women's Fashion, 1850-1920</u>, Kent, OH: The Kent State University Press, 2003.

Dann, Norman K. <u>Cousins of Reform</u>, Hamilton: Log Cabin Books, 2013.

Dann, Norman K. <u>Greene Smith and the Wild Life</u>, Hamilton: Log Cabin Books, 2015.

Fairbanks, A.W. <u>Emma Willard and Her Pupils</u>, New York: Mrs. Russell Sage, 1898.

Fitzhugh, George. <u>Cannibals All!</u> Cambridge: Harvard University Press, 1960. Originally published in 1857.

Green Mountain and Finger Lakes National Forests Notes, Late Winter, 2004.

Gordon, Ann D., ed. <u>The Selected Papers of Elizabeth Cady Stanton and Susan B. Anthony</u>, vols. I-IV. New Brunswick: Rutgers University Press, 1997.

Griffith, Elizabeth. <u>In Her Own Right: The Life of Elizabeth Cady Stanton</u>, New York: Oxford University Press, 1984.

Huntsinger, Laura M. <u>Harvard Portraits</u>, Cambridge: Harvard University Press, 1936.

James, Edward T., ed. <u>Notable American Women: A Biographical Dictionary, 1607-1950</u>. Cambridge: Harvard University Press, 1971.

Leakey, Richard E. and Roger Lewin. <u>Origins</u>, New York: E.P. Dutton, 1977.

Lutz, Alma. <u>Susan B. Anthony</u>, Zenger Publishing Co., 1975.

Marshall, Verne M. <u>The Roses of Geneva</u>, Interlaken, NY: Windswept Press, 1993.

McHenry, Robert. <u>Famous American Women</u>, New York: Dover Publications, 1980.

Miller, Elizabeth Smith. <u>In The Kitchen</u>, New York: Henry Holt and Company, revised edition, 1903. Originally published in 1875.

Morton, Edwin. <u>Verse</u>, Morges, Switzerland: Lavanchy, 1889.

Nies, Judith. <u>Nine Women</u>, Berkeley: University of California Press, 2002.

Perry, Mark. <u>Lift Up Thy Voice: The Grimké Family's Journey from Slaveholders to Civil Rights Leaders</u>, New York: Penguin Books, 2001.

Sernett, Milton C. <u>Cradle of the Breed</u>, Cazenovia, New York: Milton C. Sernett, 2010.

Smith, Catherine and Cynthia Greig. <u>Women in Pants</u>, New York: Harry N. Abrams, 2003.

Smith, Warren Hunting. <u>Hobart and William Smith: The History of Two Colleges</u>, Geneva, NY: Hobart + Wm Smith, 1972.

Snyder, Charles McCool. <u>Dr. Mary Walker: The Little Lady in Pants</u>, Salem, New Hampshire: Ayer Company, 1985.

Stauffer, John. <u>The Black Hearts of Men: Radical Abolitionists and the Transformation of Race</u>, Cambridge: Harvard University Press, 2002.

Stanton, Elizabeth Cady, Susan B. Anthony and Matilda Joslyn Gage, eds. <u>History of Woman Suffrage</u>, vol. 1, Rochester: Charles Mann, 1889.

Stanton, Theodore and Harriot Stanton Blatch, eds. <u>Elizabeth Cady Stanton As Revealed in Her Letters, Diary, and Reminiscences</u>, New York: Harper + Brothers, 1922.

Sterling, Dorothy, ed. <u>We Are Your Sisters: Black Women in the Nineteenth Century</u>, 2013.

Wellman, Judith. <u>The Road to Seneca Falls</u>, Chicago: University of Chicago Press, 2004.

Willard, Frances E. <u>Dress and Vice</u>, Chicago: Woman's Temperance Publication Association, n.d.

Woolson, Abba Goold, ed. <u>Dress Reform: A Series of Lectures Delivered in Boston, on Dress as it Affects the Health of Women</u>, Boston: Roberts Brothers, 1874.

PERIODICALS

Blatch, Harriot Stanton, co-author, "Interesting People," in <u>The American Magazine</u>, vol. Lxii, May to October, 1911.

Blatch, Harriot Stanton. "Mrs. Elizabeth Smith Miller," in <u>The American Magazine</u>, vol. 73, July 1911, 308-310.

Bloomer, Amelia. "True History of the So-Called Bloomer Costume," <u>Religio-Philosophical Journal</u>, Dec. 28, 1889.

Curtis, Mary. "Amelia Bloomer's Curious Costume," <u>American History Illustrated</u>, vol. 13, no. 3, June 1978, 10-15.

Fischer, Gayle Veronica. "She Ought to Be a <u>Female-man</u>: Dress Reform in the Oneida Community, 1848-1879," in <u>Mid-America: An Historical Review</u>, Fall, 1995.

Frye, Marilyn. "Oppression" in <u>Feminist Frontiers</u>, Richardson et. al., eds. Boston: McGraw Hill, 2004.

Huff, Robert A. "Anne Miller and the Geneva Political Equality Club, 1897-1912," <u>New York History</u>, 65 (October, 1984) 325-48.

Huff, Robert A. "Elizabeth Smith Miller: The Geneva Years," Geneva Historical Society.

Kesselman, Amy. "The 'Freedom Suit': Feminism and Dress Reform in the United States, 1848-1875," in <u>Gender and Society</u>, vol. 5, no. 4, Dec., 1991, 495-510.

Kotary, Kimberly. "To Vote or Not to Vote" in <u>Madison County Heritage</u>, no. 22, 1997.

Lowrey, George and Dana Cooke, "Hobart and the Women's Suffrage Debate," <u>The Pulteney St. Survey</u>, Summer, 1997.

Miller, Elizabeth Smith. "Reflections on Woman's Dress, and the Record of a Personal Experience," <u>Arena</u>, Sept. 1892, pp. 491-495.

Poultry World, 1873, vol. 2-4.

Preston, Ann. Address at the Woman's Rights Convention, 1852 in The Lily, August, 1852.

Riegel, Robert E. "The Spirit of the Feminist Movement in 1869," in The Mississippi Valley Historical Review, vol. 49, no. 3, Dec. 1962, 485-496.

Riegel, Robert E. "Women's Clothes and Women's Rights," in American Quarterly, vol. 15, no. 3, 390-401.

Sherman, Charlotte. "Thank You, Elizabeth Smith Miller," Broome County Historical Society Newsletter, Spring, 1996.

NEWSPAPERS

Auburn Weekly Bulletin, April 19, 1894.

Brooklyn Eagle, Aug. 18, 1851; Feb. 19, 1853; Feb. 17, 1853; Nov. 15, 1852; Jan. 14, 1857.

Buffalo Republic, Nov. 1851.

Day Lily, unpublished newspaper, Dorothy H. Willsey, ed., Peterboro, NY, vol. 1, no. 1, 1, 1983; vol. 1, no. 2, 1983; vol. 1, no. 3, 1983; vol. 1, no. 5, 1983.

Democratic Business, May 25, 1911.

Fredonia Censor, June 17, 1851.

Geneva Advertiser Gazette, Feb. 7, 1896; Oct. 25, 1906.

Illustrated London News, Sept. 13, 1851.

International Monthly, Nov. 1851.

Marcellus Observer, Oct. 12, 2005; Sept. 16, 1868.

Oneida Daily Dispatch, Nov. 28, 2009; May 29, 1914; Sept. 8, 2009; July 20, 1981; July 23, 1982; Aug. 21, 1868.

Oneida Democratic Union, Jan. 20, 1910.

Ontario County Times, Feb. 21, 1917.

Oswego Palladium, Dec. 11, 1890.

Philadelphia Inquirer, Aug. 29, 1892.

Rochester Evening Express, Sept. 8, 1868.

Women in Motion, Sept. 2007.

The Geneva News, Jan. 20, 1910.

The Lily, Aug. 1852; June 1851; March 1851; April 1852; Jan. 1852; April 1851; Feb. 1851.

The New York Times, Feb. 8, 2004; Jan. 31, 1852; April 13, 1853; Oct. 15, 1852; Sept. 7, 1876; Feb. 8, 2004.

<u>The Sibyl</u>, July, 1857; Feb., 1857; Jan. 15, 1857; Oct. 1, 1857.

<u>The Standard</u>, May 31, 1877.

<u>The World</u>, Jan. 3, 1895.

<u>Syracuse Daily Courier</u>, June 18, 1857.

<u>Syracuse Herald</u>, May 24, 1911; May 27, 1911.

<u>Syracuse Herald American</u>, March 1, 1998.

<u>Syracuse Journal</u>, June 2, 1911.

<u>Syracuse Post Standard</u>, Nov. 19, 1998; Aug. 1, 2010; Sept. 3, 2007; Feb. 17, 2011; Jan. 4, 1908.

<u>Syracuse Standard</u>, April 18, 1851.

<u>Utica Phoenix</u>, April, 2010.

Web Sites

memory.loc.gov/cgi-bin/query/S?ammem/rbcmillerbib:
@FIELD(AUTHOR+@od1(+miller,+elizabeth+smith+))

http://libwww.syr.edu/digital/exhibits/g/GerritSmith/esm.htm

http://campus.hws.edu/NEW/pss/scrap.html

www.spirithistory.com/78watk.html

www.hws.edu

www.loc.gov/exhibits/treasurers/

www.hws.edu/NEW/pss/coleburn.html

www.hws.edu/NEW/pss/scrap.html

www.liberty-resources.org

http://www.neh.gov/news/humanities/2006-05/suffragists.html

www.lochlandinc.org

www.the-review.com/news/article/4473390

www.wwhp.org/Resources/Woman'sRights/call.html

http://www.library.rochester.edu/index.cfm?page=1800

www.winningthevote.org/ESMiller.html

www.winningthevote.org/AFMiller.html

www.alexanderstreet6.com/wasm/wasmrestricted/dress

Unpublished MS

Blatch, Harriot Stanton, "Address in Memory of Anne Fitzhugh Miller, unpublished manuscript, March 5, 1912.

Miller, Blandina Dudley, "Miller Genealogy," unpublished manuscript, no date.

Staley-Mays, Robert. "Amelia and Her Bloomers," unpublished manuscript, July 1980.

Staley-Mays, Robert. "A Place in History for the Women of the United States," address to the Elizabeth Cady Stanton Foundation, Oct. 27, 1979.

Index

abolition 11
Academy of Design, NYC 23
Adams, John 43
Addams, Jane 158
Adler, Felix 177
Albany, NY 29,60,84,87
American Anti-Slavery Association 12
American Equal Rights Association 162
Anthony, Mary 165
Anthony, Susan B. 99,114,143,154-156,158,165,171,182
antislavery movement, the 13
Auburn, NY 155,160
Auburn Theological Seminary 18
Austin, Harriet Newell 145
Backus, Azel 7
Backus, Frederick 7
Backus, Rebecca Fitzhugh 7
Backus, Wealtha 7,8,
Battle of the Crater 93
Belleville, NJ 46
Berlin, Germany 90,91
Birdhouse, the 108
Birney, James G. 14,47
Blackwell, Alice Stone 171
Blackwell, Elizabeth 116
Blackwell, Henry 34
Blackwell House 116
Blatch, Harriot Stanton 73
Bloomer, Amelia 126,128,129,132-135,138-142
bloomers 124-150
Bloomer Convention 128
Bloomer Girls 128
Boston, MA 14,30,50,77,84,89,180
Boston University School of Medicine 131
Bosworth, Laura 81
Brandeis, Louis 76
Bridge, Anne Palfrey 107
Brilton, Margaret 99
Brooks, Preston 44
Brown, John 14,88,118-120,152,154,182
Brown, Mary 146
Buffalo Mines, Ltd. 184
Bunner House, Oswego 94
Burrall, Mrs. Charles S. 178
Calkins, Caleb 23,40,181

Calvinism 59
Carroll, Maj. Charles 8
Catt, Carrie Chapman 171
Cayuga Chief 139,140
Caywood Point 110
Cazenovia, NY 14,26,28,31,39,44,45,84,87,153
Chase, Salmon P. 43
Cherry Valley, NY 28
Chicago, IL 94
Chimes Calendar 85
cholera 8
Christmas rose 178,179
Christy Minstrels, the 67
cirrhosis 57
Civil War, the 93,152,154,159
Clapp, Mrs. H.K. 165
Clifton Springs, NY 94,166
Clinton, Senator Hillary Rodham 183
Clinton, NY 7,18,19
Cochrane, John 117
Colosseum, Rome 90
Common Place Book 36
'College on the Hill' 7
Confucious 104
Congregational Church, Brookton, NY 170
Constitution of the Colony of New Jersey (1776) 175
consumption 46
Cook, Elizabeth 170
Cooper Institute 158
Cornell University 102,107
Cottage Across the Brook 147
Coudray, Louis 90
Coues, Elliot 102
Council Bluffs, IA 139
County Cork 89
Cox, Rev. Dr. S.H. 160
Dansville, NY 145
Darwin, Charles 158
Day Lily 147
Declaration of Sentiments 162
Dixwell, Epes S. 47,48,76
Dixwell, Susan 48
Douglas, Stephen A. 43
Douglass, Frederick 14,59,131,152,154,182

Dr. R.T. Trall's Hydropathic College 145
Dresden, Germany 90,91
dress reformers 123.135
  Dress Reform Association 139
Dutch Reformed Church (Utica, NY) 28
Eastman, Rev. Annis Ford 170
Eastman, Rev. Samuel 180
Edwards, John B. 37,40,48
Elizabeth Smith Miller Project, the 146
Elizabeth Smith Miller Study Club 158
Emerson, Ralph Waldo 104,170
England 48
Epes Sargent Dixwell's Latin School, Boston 47
Equal Rights Association 154
Erie Canal, the 114
Evans Academy 18
Fanning, Prudy 146
Fayetteville, NY 18
Female Anti-Slavery Society (Hamilton,
  NY) 154
Field Ornithology 102
Finney, Charles Grandison 59,62
First Presbyterian Church, Brooklyn 160
Fitzhugh, Col. William 8
Fitzhugh, George 134
Florence, Italy 90
Forten, Charlotte 13
Forten, James 12,13,89
Forten, Sarah 15
Fossenvue 32,81,100-106
Camp, The 106,108,109
Queen's Castle, the 107,109,110
Fossett's Point 101,104
Fowler, James 107
Free Church of Peterboro 62,63,117,154
Frister, Noah 94
Frothingham, Octavius Brooks 43,117-121
Fuertes, Louis Agassiz 102
Gage, Matilda Joslyn 156
Garrison, William Lloyd 14,76
Geary, John (Pennsylvania Governor) 158
Geneva Academy 115
Geneva College 115,116
  Medical Institute 116
Geneva Falls 8
Geneva, NY vi,32,44,50,56,93-
  99,113,115,152,171
Geneva Advertiser Gazette 172,178
Geneva Opera House 116
Geneva Political Equality Club 105,114,
  157,159,163-166,168-170,178

Genoa, Italy 90
Germantown, PA 23
Germany 48
Giddings, Joshua R. 43
Glasgow, Scotland 90
Glen Haven Water Cure 139,145
Golden Rule, the 113,185
Goodell, William 14
Gordon, Charles "Chinese" George 104
Green Mountain and Finger Lakes National
  Forests 109
Green, Rev. Beriah 14,30
Grimké, Sarah 48,49,62
Hagerstown, MD 89
Hamburg, Germany 90
Hamilton College 7,18,60
Hamilton, NY 18,84,153
Hampton, NY 8,12
Hannah Whitall's Quaker school 20
Harlow, Ralph Volney 119
Harper Ferry, VA 118
Harvard College 36,48,117
Harvard Divinity School 117
Hasbrouck, Lydia Sayer 127,131,139
Hegel, Georg Wilhelm Friedrich 104
History of Woman Suffrage 123,151
Hobart College 115
Hobart College Chaplain Rev. Joseph Alex-
  ander Leighton 159,160
Hobart College President Eliphalet Nott Pot-
  ter 160
Hobart & William Smith Colleges 28,107
Holland 48
Holmes, Oliver Wendell 158
Holstein cattle 48,95
Homer, NY 138
Homosassa, FL 94
Honeoye, NY 166
Howe, Kate L. 33
Hoomi, Koot 104
Huff, Robert 152
Hugo, Victor 158
Hume, David 104
hypochondria 71
In The Kitchen 23,75-80,82
"In The Kitchen Tea" 149
Ireland 89
Ithaca, NY 102
Jackson, James Caleb 139,145
Jackson, Mercy B., M.D. 133
Jay, NY Gov. John 28

Jenner, Edward 9
Jesus Christ 18,19,31
Jim Crow laws 185
Kant, Immanuel 104
Keats, John 104
Kellogg, Rev. Dr. Hiram H. 18
Kelty, Betsey 9,19,21,30,32,42,45,49,65,
  66,81,113
King, Caroline Freedom 18
King William I 91
Lafayette, NY 18
Lake Ontario 87
Lamb, Charles 104
Laws of Life and Journal of Health 145
League of Women Voters 184
Leakey, Richard 101
Leaning Tower of Pisa 90
Ledyard, Nan 71
Lee & Shepherd 77
"Les Miserables" 158
Lincoln, Abraham 158
Liverpool, England 89
Livingston County, NY 8
"Lizzie Smith Fashions" 149
Lizzy Smith Project, the 147,150
Lochland 32,36,44,50,56,93-101,106,109,
  151,152,155,160,163,170,171,177,184
Locke, John 104
London, England 13, 89-91,138,178
Loomis, Henry H. 115
Luce, Jody 148,149
Lucerne, Switzerland 90
Luxembourg 63
Lyon, France 89
Madison County Bank 28,31,40
Madison County Historical Society 149
Madison County Task Force Against Do-
  mestic Violence 146
mastitis 26
Maryland 7
measles 11
Meehan, Charles 170
Mendelssohn, Felix 158
Men's League for Woman Suffrage 178
Millais, John Everett 104
Miller, Anne 'Nannie' Fitzhugh 44,50-56,91,
  102,105,107,108,146,152,156,160,165,
  170,171,176
Miller, Charles Dudley 14,27-37,40,43,48,
  50,51,57,62,90,91,95,96,127,141,154,177
Miller, Charles Dudley II 48,49,89-91,95

Miller, Dudley 44
Miller, Gerrit 'Gat' Smith 44-
  48,54,76,89,95,99,119,121,180
Miller House at William Smith College
  116,180,184
Miller, Hon. Morris S. 28
Miller, Maria Bleeker 28
Miller, Susan D. 99
Miller, William Fitzhugh 43,49,50,51,107
Mills, Edwin M. 184
Mills, Harriet May 162,170
Montgomery, Mrs. W.A. 157
Morton, Edwin 74,77,88
Mott, Lucretia Coffin 13,125
Mr. Punch's Victorian Era 136,137
Mygatt, 'Minny' 18,23
Naples, Italy 90
National Guard, the 31
National Republican Convention
  Chicago, 1868 154
National Soccer Hall of Fame 47
National American Woman Suffrage Associa-
  tion 155,162,170
National American Woman Suffrage Associ-
  ation Convention
  (1897) 116
  (1907) 171
  (1910) 171
  (1911) 180
National Collaborative for Women's History
  Sites 184
National Women's Rights Convention
  Seneca Falls, 1848 13,125,132,151,154
  Worcester, MA, 1850 154
  Syracuse, 1852 128
  Pittsfield, MA 1853 160
National Women's Rights History Project
  Act 183
National Women's Suffrage Association 154
Negro Universities Press 121
New England Women's Club 132
  Dress Reform Committee 132
New Harmony community 128
New Orleans Times-Democrat 155
New Jersey 136
New York Anti-Slavery Society 154
New York City 29,48-50,54,55,77,
  84,88,94,95,117,145,158
New York State Association Opposed to the
  Extension of Suffrage to Women 159
New York State Constitution 176

New York State Governor's Commission Honoring the Achievements of Women 149
New York State Judiciary Committee 174
New York State Woman Suffrage Association 155,162,166,171
New York Women's Equality Coalition 183
New York State Thruway 88
New York Times 135
Nova Scotia 37
Noyes, John Humphrey 128
O'Donnell, Miriam 148
Oneida Community, the 128,144
Oneida Co. Court of Common Pleas 28
Oneida Nation, the 14,181
Ontario County 154
Ontario County Times 180
Ontario County Woman Suffrage Association Convention (1910) 171
Orange County, NY
Osborne, Thomas Matt 160
Oswego, NY 36,37,40,44,48,87,94
Owen, Robert 128
Panic of 1837 21,30
Pankhurst, Emmeline 170
Pantheon, Rome 90
Paris, France 49,90,91
Park Church, Elmira 180
Pelzer, George 170
Peterboro Historical Society 150
Parker House Hotel, Boston 89
Peterboro Land Office 23,31,74,83,181
Peterboro, NY 7,12,14,18,21,23,29,40,55,70,87,88,93,94,108,113,141,151,153,154
Peterboro Village Green home 42,44
Peterboro Women's Baseball Club 146
Petersburg, VA 93
Phelps, NY 166
Philadelphia, PA 12,13,20,21,22,23,84,114,123,127
Phyllis Wheatley Club 155
piazza party 156,170,171,178
Pisa, Italy 90
Plato 104
Powell, Harriet 60,116,117,182
Presbyterian Church, Peterboro 54,60,61
Predmore, Lydia 105
Preston, Dr. Ann 153
Quaker families 23,127
raisin stoner 79

Raritan Bay, NJ 44
Reform Era 59,127,159
Reorganized Church of Jesus Christ of Latter Day Saints 128
rheumatic fever 50
Richfield Springs 10
Rochester, Col. Nathan 8
Rochester, NY 7,8,12,14,20,68,87,114
Rome, Italy 90
Rome, NY 84
Rose, Elizabeth A. 178
Ross, Elizabeth 116
Roosevelt, Theodore 159
Ruskin, John 104
Russell, Melvina 81
S.S. Seward Institute 127
St. Peter's Basilica, Rome 90
Sanborn, Franklin Benjamin 88
Savino, New York State Senator Diane 183
Schenectady, NY 8,30,155
Schmidt, Nathaniel 102,180
Schoder, Prof. Ernest 170
Second Great Awakening, the 59
"Secret Six," the 88,121
Seneca County Courier 139,140
Seneca Falls, NY 13,82,125,138
Seneca Lake 32,44,101,106
Shaw, Anna Howard 170
Sherrill, NY 144
Sidney, Sir Philip 104
Slaughter, U.S. Representative Louise M. 183
smallpox 8,9
Smith, Ann Carroll Fitzhugh 51
Smith, Ann Fitzhugh 7-15,18,19,21,22,25,28,29,31,34,40,45,46,50,55,65,68,70,77,81,88,89,94,99,113,114,136,153,156
Smith, Bessie 89,93,94,99
Smithfield Community Association 150
Smith, Fitzhugh 9,10,11,17
Smith, Gerrit 7,8,9,10,14,15,16,21,28-32,36-38,42-44,50,55,59,60,61,65,68-74,82,87-91,93-96,99,113,116-121,125,129,133,141,152,153,156,181
Smith, Greene 25,46,71,72,88-90,93-96,102,108,117-121,135
Smith Mansion 8,12,27,40,41,93,98,116,119,120
Smith, Nan 10,11
Smith, Peter 8,27
Smith, William 23,115,116
Snyder, Emily Dilworth 107

Spencer, Anna Garlin 180
Spinoza, Baruch 104
Stafford-Blake, Mary J. 131
Stanton, Elizabeth Cady 11,13,47,48,
    59,63,67,72,75,117,123,124,125,134,138,
    140-141,143,151,153,154,156-158,160,
    176,181,182
Stanton, Henry B. 14
Stevens, Alexander H. 43
Stewardson, Langdon C. 115,180
Stewardson, Mrs. Langdon C. 169
Stone, Lucy 34,129
Stowe, Harriet Beecher 158
Strasbourg, France 91
Strange, James J. 128
Strangites, the 128
Sullivan St. home, Cazenovia (see Truax
    House)
Sumner, Charles 43
Sydenham chorea 49
Syracuse, NY 84,141
Syracuse University 119
Tennyson, Alfred 158
The Grove 30,31
The Liberator 14
The Lily 126,138-140
The North Star 14
The Revolution 154, 158
The Sibyl 131,139
Troy Female Seminary 18
Troy, NY 18
Truax House 39,45
Tubman, Harriet 14,59
tuberculosis 25,72
Twain, Mark 76
"Uncle Tom's Cabin" 158
U.S. Congress 28,42,67
U.S. Department of Agriculture Forest
    Service 109
Union College 28
Utica, NY 28,49
Vaughn. Hester 158
Ver Planck, Ruth Leslie 105,107
Verse Book (Smith family) 15,32,85
Virgin Mary, the 63
Walker, Dr. Mary 135,141
Wampsville, NY 23,87
Warwick, NY 127
Washington, D.C. 42,43,68,89,146
Water Cure Journal, the 128
Weld, Angelina 46,48

Weld, Theodore 14,44,46
Weld School 44,46-48,62
Whitall, Hannah 20
Whittier, John Greenleaf 158
Wickham, Miss Bell 17
Wigglesworth, Martha 47
Wigglesworth, Suzan 47
Wilkerson, Samuel 53
Willard Asylum for the Chronic Insane 114
Willard, Emma 18
Willard. Frances 133
Willard, NY 114
William Smith College for Women
    23,115,157,178
Williams, Sylvanie 155
Willis, Dr. Frederick H. 170
Willsey, Dorothy H. 146,148
Woodbury, Margaret 54
Woolson, Abba Goold 129,132
Woman's Christian Temperance Union 133
Woman's Social and Political Union (Britain)
    170
Woman Suffrage Association of America 155
Women's History Month 183
Working Woman's Association 158
World Anti-Slavery Conference, 1840 13
Young Ladies' Domestic Seminary 18
Young Ladies' Saturday Morning Club of
    Boston 76
Zurich, Switzerland 90,91

About the Author

This is the sixth book by Norman K. Dann, Ph.D.

He was born in Providence, RI in 1940. After graduating from Mt. Pleasant High School, he spent three years in the U.S. Navy as an aviation electronics technician.

He earned a bachelor of arts degree in psychology from Alderson-Broaddus College in Philippi, WV and a master of arts in Political Science from the University of Rhode Island.

He was graduated from Syracuse University in 1974 with a Ph.D. in In-

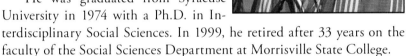

terdisciplinary Social Sciences. In 1999, he retired after 33 years on the faculty of the Social Sciences Department at Morrisville State College.

In retirement, Norm has specialized in research and writing on the abolition movement, with several articles and book reviews in publication. He published his first book, *When We Get to Heaven: Runaway Slaves on the Road to Peterboro*, in 2008. His second book in 2009 was a full biography that capped more than 15 years of research on abolitionist Gerrit Smith. It is titled *Practical Dreamer: Gerrit Smith and the Crusade for Social Reform*. His third book, *Whatever It Takes: The Antislavery Movement and the Tactics of Gerrit Smith*, came out in 2011. His fourth book, *Cousins of Reform: Elizabeth Cady Stanton and Gerrit Smith*, was published in 2013. His fifth book, *Greene Smith and the WildLife: The Story of Peterboro's Avid Outdoorsman*, was published in 2015. All titles are from Log Cabin Books of Hamilton, NY.

His other interests include sterling silver craft work. He creates jewelry pieces and specializes in silver plaques. One plaque was a centerpiece of Madison County's bicentennial celebration in 2006. Norm also enjoys archery hunting for whitetail deer and maintains a large vegetable garden. He cultivates hop plants for display and sale through the annual Madison County Hop Fest.

Norm has dedicated his retirement to communicating the importance of local history regarding abolition. He is a member of the Peterboro-based Smithfield Community Association and helps manage the group's annual fund-raiser, Civil War Weekend. He is a founding member of the National Abolition Hall of Fame & Museum.

OTHER BOOKS BY NORMAN K. DANN

When We Get to Heaven:
Runaway Slaves on the Road to Peterboro
(2008)

Practical Dreamer:
Gerrit Smith and the Crusade for Social Reform
(2009)

Whatever It Takes:
The Antislavery Movement
and the Tactics of Gerrit Smith
(2011)

Cousins of Reform:
Elizabeth Cady Stanton and Gerrit Smith
(2013)

Greene Smith and the WildLife:
The Story of Peterboro's Avid Outdoorsman
(2015)

All titles are from
LOG CABIN BOOKS of Hamilton, NY.
www.logcabinbooks.com